HILAIRE BELLOC

THE AFTERMATH *or* GLEANINGS FROM A BUSY LIFE

CALLED UPON THE OUTER COVER

FOR PURPOSES OF SALE

CALIBAN'S GUIDE TO LETTERS

By H. B.

LONDON
DUCKWORTH & CO.,
3 HENRIETTA STREET, W.C.

TO

CATHERINE, MRS. CALIBAN,

BUT FOR WHOSE FRUITFUL SUGGESTION, EVER-READY SYMPATHY, POWERS OF OBSERVATION, KINDLY CRITICISM, UNFLINCHING COURAGE, CATHOLIC LEARNING, AND NONE THE LESS CHRISTIAN PRINCIPLE,

THIS BOOK MIGHT AS WELL NOT HAVE BEEN WRITTEN;

IT IS DEDICATED

BY

HER OBEDIENT AND GRATEFUL SERVANT AND FRIEND IN AFFLICTION,

THE AUTHOR.

"*O, Man; with what tremors as of earth-begettings hast thou not wrought, O, Man!—Yet—is it utterly indeed of thee—? Did there not toil in it also that* WORLD-MAN, *or haply was there not Some Other? . . . . O, Man! knowest thou that word Some Other?*"—CARLYLE'S "Frederick the Great."

Most of these sketches are reprinted from "The Speaker," and appear in this form by the kind permission of its Editor.

ERRATA AND ADDENDA.

P. 19, line 14 (from the top), for "enteric" read "esoteric."

P. 73, second footnote, for "Sophia, Lady Gowl," read "Lady Sophia Gowl."

P. 277 (line 5 from bottom), for "the charming prospect of such a *bribe*," read "*Bride*."

P. 456, delete all references to Black-mail, *passim*.

P. 510 (line 6 from top), for "*Chou-fleur*," read "*Chauffeur*."

DIRECTION TO PRINTER.—Please print hard, strong, clear, straight, neat, clean, and well. Try and avoid those little black smudges!

PREFACE.

This work needs no apology.

Its value to the English-speaking world is two-fold. It preserves for all time, in the form of a printed book, what might have been scattered in the sheets of ephemeral publications. It is so designed that these isolated monuments of prose and verse can be studied, absorbed, and, if necessary, copied by the young aspirant to literary honours.

Nothing is Good save the Useful, and it would have been sheer vanity to have published so small a selection, whatever its merit, unless it could be made to do Something, to achieve a Result in this strenuous modern world. It will not be the fault of the book, but of the reader, if no creative impulse follows its perusal, and the student will have but himself to blame if, with such standards before him, and so lucid and thorough an analysis of modern

Literature and of its well-springs, he does not attain the goal to which the author would lead him.

The book will be found conveniently divided into sections representing the principal divisions of modern literary activity; each section will contain an introductory essay, which will form a practical guide to the subject with which it deals, and each will be adorned with one or more examples of the finished article, which, if the instructions be carefully followed, should soon be turned out without difficulty by any earnest and industrious scholar of average ability.

If the Work can raise the income of but one poor journalist, or produce earnings, no matter how insignificant, for but one of that great army which is now compelled to pay for the insertion of its compositions in the newspapers and magazines, the labour and organizing ability devoted to it will not have been in vain.

INTRODUCTION.

A Grateful Sketch of the Author's Friend (in part the producer of this book),

JAMES CALIBAN.

INTRODUCTION.

Few men have pursued more honourably, more usefully, or more successfully the career of letters than Thomas Caliban, D.D., of Winchelthorpe-on-Sea, near Portsmouth. Inheriting, as his name would imply, the grand old Huguenot strain, his father was a Merchant Taylor of the City of London, and principal manager of the Anglo-Chilian Bank; his mother the fifth daughter of K. Muller, Esq., of Brighton, a furniture dealer and reformer of note in the early forties.

The connection established between my own family and that of Dr. Caliban I purposely pass over as not germane to the ensuing pages, remarking only that the friendship, guidance, and intimacy of such a man will ever count among my chiefest treasures. Of him it may truly be written: "*He maketh them to shine like Sharon; the waters are his in Ram-Shaîd, and Gilgath praiseth him.*"

I could fill a volume of far greater contents than has this with the mere record of his every-day acts during the course of his long and active career. I must content myself, in this sketch, with a bare summary of his habitual deportment. He would rise in the morning, and after a simple but orderly toilet would proceed to family prayers, terminating the same with a hymn, of which he would himself read each verse in turn, to be subsequently chanted by the assembled household. To this succeeded breakfast, which commonly consisted of ham, eggs, coffee, tea, toast, jam, and what-not—in a word, the appurtenances of a decent table.

Breakfast over, he would light a pipe (for he did not regard indulgence in the weed as immoral, still less as un-Christian: the subtle word *ἐπιείκεια*, which he translated "sweet reasonableness," was painted above his study door—it might have served for the motto of his whole life), he would light a pipe, I say, and walk round his garden, or, if it rained, visit the plants in his conservatory.

Before ten he would be in his study, seated at a large mahogany bureau, formerly the property of Sir Charles Henby, of North-chapel, and noon would still find him there, writing in his regular and legible hand the notes and manuscripts which have made him famous, or poring over an encyclopædia, the more conscientiously to review some book with which he had been entrusted.

After the hours so spent, it was his habit to take a turn in the fresh air, sometimes speaking to the gardener, and making the round of the beds; at others passing by the stables to visit his pony Bluebell, or to pat upon the head his faithful dog Ponto, now advanced in years and suffering somewhat from the mange.

To this light exercise succeeded luncheon, for him the most cheerful meal of the day. It was then that his liveliest conversation was heard, his closest friends entertained: the government, the misfortunes of foreign nations, the success of our fiscal policy, our maritime supremacy, the definition of the word "gentleman," occasionally even a little bout of theology—a thousand subjects fell into the province of his genial criticism and extensive information; to each his sound judgment and ready apprehension added some new light; nor were the ladies of the family incompetent to follow the gifted table talk of their father, husband, brother, master,* and host.†

Until the last few years the hour after lunch was occupied with a stroll upon the terrace, but latterly he would consume it before the fire in sleep, from which the servants had orders to wake him by three o'clock. At this hour he would take his hat and stick and proceed into the town, where his sunny smile and friendly salute were familiar to high and low. A visit to the L.N.C. School, a few purchases, perhaps even a call upon the vicar (for Dr. Caliban was without prejudice—the broadest of men), would be the occupation of the afternoon, from which he returned to tea in the charming drawing-room of 48, Henderson Avenue.

It was now high time to revisit his study. He was

* The governess invariably took her meals with the family.

† Miss Bowley, though practically permanently resident in the family, was still but a guest—a position which she never forgot, though Dr. Caliban forbad a direct allusion to the fact.

at work by six, and would write steadily till seven. Dinner, the pleasant conversation that succeeds it in our English homes, perhaps an innocent round game, occupied the evening till a gong for prayers announced the termination of the day. Dr. Caliban made it a point to remain the last up, to bolt the front door, to pour out his own whiskey, and to light his own candle before retiring. It was consonant with his exact and thoughtful nature, by the way, to have this candle of a patent sort, pierced down the middle to minimise the danger from falling grease; it was moreover surrounded by a detachable cylinder of glass.*

Such was the round of method which, day by day and week by week, built up the years of Dr. Caliban's life; but life is made up of little things, and, to quote a fine phrase of his own: "It is the hourly habits of a man that build up his character." He also said (in his address to the I. C. B. Y.): "Show me a man hour by hour in his own home, from the rising of the sun to his going down, and I will tell you what manner of man he is." I have always remembered the epigram, and have acted upon it in the endeavour to portray the inner nature of its gifted author.

I should, however, be giving but an insufficient picture of Dr. Caliban were I to leave the reader with no further impression of his life work, or indeed of the causes which have produced this book.

His father had left him a decent competence. He

* Such as are sold and patented by my friend Mr. Gapethorn, of 362, Fetter Lane.

lay, therefore, under no necessity to toil for his living. Nevertheless, that sense of duty, "through which the eternal heavens are fresh and strong" (Wordsworth), moved him to something more than "the consumption of the fruits of the earth" (Horace). He preached voluntarily and without remuneration for some years to the churches in Cheltenham, and having married Miss Bignor, of Winchelthorpe-on-Sea, purchased a villa in that rising southern watering-place, and received a call to the congregation, which he accepted. He laboured there till his recent calamity.

I hardly know where to begin the recital of his numerous activities in the period of thirty-five years succeeding his marriage. With the pen he was indefatigable. A man more ποικίλος—or, as he put it, many-sided—perhaps never existed. There was little he would not touch, little upon which he was not consulted, and much in which, though anonymous, he was yet a leader.

He wrote regularly, in his earlier years, for *The Seventh Monarchy*, *The Banner*, *The Christian*, *The Free Trader*, *Household Words*, *Good Words*, *The Quiver*, *Chatterbox*, *The Home Circle*, and *The Sunday Monitor*. During the last twenty years his work has continually appeared in the *Daily Telegraph*, the *Times*, the *Siècle*, and the *Tribuna*. In the last two his work was translated.

His political effect was immense, and that though he never acceded to the repeated request that he would stand upon one side or the other as a candidate for Parliament. He remained, on the contrary, to the end of his career, no more than president of a local association. It was as a speaker, writer, and preacher, that his ideas spread outwards; thousands certainly now use political phrases which they may imagine their own, but which undoubtedly sprang from his creative brain. He was perhaps not the first, but one of the first, to apply the term "Anglo-Saxon" to the English-speaking race—with which indeed he was personally connected through his relatives in New Mexico. The word "Empire" occurs in a sermon of his as early as 1869. He was contemporary with Mr. Lucas, if not before him, in the phrase, "Command of the sea": and I find, in a letter to Mrs. Gorch, written long ago in 1873, the judgment that Protection was "no longer," and the nationalization of land "not yet," within "the sphere of practical politics."

If his influence upon domestic politics was in part due to his agreement with the bulk of his fellow-citizens, his attitude in foreign affairs at least was all his own. Events have proved it wonderfully sound. A strenuous opponent of American slavery as a very young man—in 1860—he might be called, even at that age, the most prominent Abolitionist in Worcestershire, and worked indefatigably for the cause in so far as it concerned this country. A just and charitable man, he proved, after the victory of the North, one of the firmest supporters in the press of what he first termed "an Anglo-American *entente*." Yet he was not for pressing matters. He would leave the "gigantic daughter of the West" to choose her hour and time, confident in the wisdom of his daughter's judgment, and he lived to see, before his calamity fell upon him, Mr. Hanna, Mr. Roosevelt, Mr. Elihu Root, and Mr. Smoot occupying the positions they still adorn.

He comprehended Europe. It was he who prophesied of the Dual Monarchy (I believe in the *Contemporary Review*), that "the death of Francis Joseph would be the signal for a great upheaval"; he that applied to Italy the words "clericalism is the enemy"; and he that publicly advised the withdrawal of our national investments from the debt of Spain—"a nation in active decay." He cared not a jot when his critics pointed out that Spanish fours had risen since his advice no less than 20 per cent., while our own consols had fallen by an equal amount. "The kingdom I serve," he finely answered, "knows nothing of the price of stock." And indeed the greater part of his fortune was in suburban rents, saving a small sum unfortunately adventured in Shanghai Telephones.

Russia he hated as the oppressor of Finland and Poland, for oppression he loathed and combatted wherever it appeared; nor had Mr. Arthur Balfour a stronger supporter than he when that statesman, armed only in the simple manliness of an English Christian and Freeman, combatted and destroyed the terrorism that stalked through Ireland.

Of Scandinavia he knew singularly little, but that little was in its favour; and as for the German

Empire, his stanzas to Prince Bismarck, and his sermon on the Emperor's recent visit, are too well known to need any comment here. To Holland he was, until recently, attracted. Greece he despised.

Nowhere was this fine temper of unflinching courage and sterling common sense more apparent than in the great crisis of the Dreyfus case. No man stood up more boldly, or with less thought of consequence, for Truth and Justice in this country. He was not indeed the chairman of the great meeting in St. James' Hall, but his peroration was the soul of that vast assemblage. "England will yet weather the storm. . . ." It was a true prophecy, and in a sense a confession of Faith.

There ran through his character a vein of something steady and profound, which inspired all who came near him with a sense of quiet persistent *strength.* This, with an equable, unfailing pressure, restrained or controlled whatever company surrounded him. It was like the regular current of a full but silent tide, or like the consistent power of a good helmsman. It may be called his *personal force.* To most men and women of our circle, that force was a sustenance and a blessing; to ill-regulated or worldly men with whom he might come in contact, it acted as a salutary irritant, though rarely to so intense a degree as to give rise to scenes. I must unfortunately except the case of the Rural Dean of Bosham, whose notorious excess was the more lamentable from the fact that the Council of the *S.P.C.A.* is strictly non-sectarian, and whose excuse that the ink-pot was not thrown but brushed aside is, to speak plainly, a tergiversation.

The recent unhappy war in South Africa afforded an excellent opportunity for the exercise of the qualities I mean. He was still active and alert; still guiding men and maidens during its worse days. His tact was admirable. He suffered from the acute divisions of his congregation, but he suffered in powerful silence; and throughout those dark-days his sober *necquid nimis** was like a keel and ballast for us all.

A young radical of sorts was declaiming at his table one evening against the Concentration Camp. Dr. Caliban listened patiently, and at the end of the harangue said gently, "Shall we join the ladies?" The rebuke was not lost.†

On another occasion, when some foreigner was reported in the papers as having doubted Mr. Brodrick's figures relative to the numbers of the enemy remaining in the field, Dr. Caliban said with quiet dignity, "It is the first time I have heard the word of an English gentleman doubted."

It must not be imagined from these lines that he defended the gross excesses of the London mob—especially in the matter of strong waters—or that he wholly approved of our policy. "Peace in our time, *Oh, Lord!*" was his constant cry, and against militarism he thundered fearlessly. I have heard him

* Petronius.

† The Ladies were Mrs. Caliban, Miss Rachel and Miss Alethēia Caliban, Miss Bowley, Miss Goucher, and Lady Robinson.

apply to it a word that never passed his lips in any other connection—the word DAMNABLE.

On the details of the war, the policy of annexation, the advisability of frequent surrenders, the high salaries of irregulars, and the employment of national scouts, he was silent. In fine, one might have applied to him the strong and simple words of Lord Jacobs, in his Guildhall speech.* One main fact stood out—he hated warfare. He was a man of peace.

The tall, broad figure, inclining slightly to obesity, the clear blue northern eyes, ever roaming from point to point as though seeking for grace, the familiar soft wideawake, the long full white beard, the veined complexion and dark-gloved hands, are now, alas, removed from the sphere they so long adorned.

Dr. Caliban's affliction was first noticed by his family at dinner on the first of last September—a date which fell by a strange and unhappy coincidence on a Sunday. For some days past Miss Goucher had remarked his increasing volubility; but on this fatal evening, in spite of all the efforts of his wife and daughters, he continued to speak, without interruption, from half-past seven to a quarter-past nine; and again, after a short interval, till midnight, when he fell into an uneasy sleep, itself full of mutterings. His talk had seemed now a sermon, now the reminiscence of some leading article, now a monologue, but the whole quite incoherent, though delivered with passionate energy; nor was it the least dis-

* "It is enough for me that I am an Englishman."

tressing feature of his malady that he would tolerate no reply, nay, even the gentlest assent drove him into paroxysms of fury.

Next day he began again in the manner of a debate at the local Liberal Club, soon lapsing again into a sermon, and anon admitting snatches of strange songs into the flow of his words. Towards eleven he was apparently arguing with imaginary foreigners, and shortly afterwards the terrible scene was ended by the arrival of a medical man of his own persuasion.

It is doubtful whether Dr. Caliban will ever be able to leave Dr. Charlbury's establishment, but all that can be done for him in his present condition is lovingly and ungrudgingly afforded. There has even been provided for him at considerable expense, and after an exhaustive search, a companion whose persistent hallucination it is that he is acting as private secretary to some leader of the Opposition, and the poor wild soul is at rest.

Such was the man who continually urged upon me the necessity of compiling some such work as that which now lies before the reader. He had himself intended to produce a similar volume, and had he done so I should never have dared to enter the same field; but I feel that in his present incapacity I am, as it were, fulfilling a duty when I trace in these few pages the plan which he so constantly counselled, and with such a man counsels were commands. If I may be permitted to dwell upon the feature more especially his own in this Guide, I will point to the section " On Vivid Historical Literature in its Application to Modern Problems," and furthermore, to the section "On the Criticism and Distinction of Works Attributed to Classical Authors." In the latter case the examples chosen were taken from his own large collection; for it was a hobby of his to purchase as bargains manuscripts and anonymous pamphlets which seemed to him to betray the hand of some master. Though I have been compelled to differ from my friend, and cannot conscientiously attribute the specimens I have chosen to William Shakespeare or to Dean Swift, yet I am sure the reader will agree with me that the error into which Dr. Caliban fell was that of no ordinary mind.

Finally, let me offer to his family, and to his numerous circle, such apologies as may be necessary for the differences in style, and, alas, I fear, sometimes in mode of thought, between the examples which I have chosen as models for the student and those which perhaps would have more powerfully attracted the sympathies of my preceptor himself. I am well aware that such a difference is occasionally to be discovered. I can only plead in excuse that men are made in very different ways, and that the disciple cannot, even if he would, forbid himself a certain measure of self-development. Dr. Caliban's own sound and broad ethics would surely have demanded it of no one, and I trust that this solemn reference to his charity and genial toleration will put an end to the covert attacks which some of those who should have been the strongest links between us have seen fit to make in the provincial and religious press.

DIVISION I.

REVIEWING.

REVIEWING.

The ancient and honourable art of Reviewing is, without question, the most important branch of that great calling which we term the "Career of Letters."

As it is the most important, so also it is the first which a man of letters should learn. It is at once his shield and his weapon. A thorough knowledge of Reviewing, both theoretical and applied, will give a man more popularity or power than he could have attained by the expenditure of a corresponding energy in any one of the liberal professions, with the possible exception of Municipal politics.

It forms, moreover, the foundation upon which all other literary work may be said to repose. Involving, as it does, the reading of a vast number of volumes, and the thorough mastery of a hundred wholly different subjects; training one to rapid, conclusive judgment, and to the exercise of a kind of immediate power of survey, it vies with cricket in forming the character of an Englishman. It is interesting to know that Charles Hawbuck was for some years principally occupied in Reviewing; and to this day some of our most important men will write, nay, and sign, reviews, as the press of the country testifies upon every side.

It is true that the sums paid for this species of

literary activity are not large, and it is this fact which has dissuaded some of our most famous novelists and poets of recent years from undertaking Reviewing of any kind. But the beginner will not be deterred by such a consideration, and he may look forward, by way of compensation, to the ultimate possession of a large and extremely varied library, the accumulation of the books which have been given him to review. I have myself been presented with books of which individual volumes were sometimes worth as much as forty-two shillings to buy.

Having said so much of the advantages of this initial and fundamental kind of writing, I will proceed to a more exact account of its dangers and difficulties, and of the processes inherent to its manufacture.

It is clear, in the first place, that the Reviewer must regard herself as the servant of the public, and of her employer; and service, as I need hardly remind her (or him), has nothing in it dishonourable. We were all made to work, and often the highest in the land are the hardest workers of all. This character of service, of which Mr. Ruskin has written such noble things, will often lay the Reviewer under the necessity of a sharp change of opinion, and nowhere is the art a better training in morals and application than in the habit it inculcates of rapid and exact obedience, coupled with the power of seeing every aspect of a thing, and of insisting upon that particular aspect which will give most satisfaction to the commonwealth.

It may not be uninstructive if I quote here the adventures of one of the truest of the many stout-hearted men I have known, one indeed who recently died in harness reviewing Mr. Garcke's article on Electrical Traction in the supplementary volumes of the *Encyclopædia Britannica*. This gentleman was once sent a book to review; the subject, as he had received no special training in it, might have deterred one less bound by the sense of duty. This book was called *The Snail: Its Habitat, Food, Customs, Virtues, Vices, and Future*. It was, as its title would imply, a monograph upon snails, and there were many fine coloured prints, showing various snails occupied in feeding on the leaves proper to each species. It also contained a large number of process blocks, showing sections, plans, elevations, and portraits of snails, as well as detailed descriptions (with diagrams) of the ears, tongues, eyes, hair, and nerves of snails. It was a comprehensive and remarkable work.

My friend (whose name I suppress for family reasons) would not naturally have cared to review this book. He saw that it involved the assumption of a knowledge which he did not possess, and that some parts of the book might require very close reading. It numbered in all 1532 pages, but this was including the index and the preface.

He put his inclinations to one side, and took the book with him to the office of the newspaper from which he had received it, where he was relieved to hear the Editor inform him that it was not necessary to review the work in any great detail. "Moreover," he added, "I don't think you need praise it too much."

On hearing this, the Reviewer, having noted down the price of the book and the name of the publisher, wrote the following words—which, by the way, the student will do well to cut out and pin upon his wall, as an excellent example of what a "short notice" should be :—

> "*The Snail: Its Habitat,* &c. Adam Charles. Pschuffer. 21s. 6d.
>
> "This is a book that will hardly add to the reputation of its author. There is evidence of detailed work, and even of conscientious research in several places, but the author has ignored or misunderstood the whole teaching of   and the special discoveries of   and what is even more remarkable in a man of Mr. Charles' standing, he advances views which were already exploded in the days of   ."

He then took an Encyclopædia and filled up the blanks with the names of three great men who appeared, according to that work, to be the leaders in this branch of natural history. His duty thus thoroughly accomplished and his mind at rest, he posted his review, and applied himself to lighter occupations.

Next day, however, the Editor telephoned to him, to the effect that the notice upon which he had spent so much labour could not be used.

"We have just received," said the Editor, "a page advertisement from Pschuffer. I would like a really good article, and you might use the book as a kind of peg on which to hang it. You might begin on the subject of snails, and make it something more like your '*Oh! my lost friend,*' which has had such a success."

On occasions such as these the beginner must remember to keep full possession of himself.

Nothing in this mortal life is permanent, and the changes that are native to the journalistic career are perhaps the most startling and frequent of all those which threaten humanity.

The Reviewer of whom I speak was as wise as he was honourable. He saw at once what was needed. He wrote another and much longer article, beginning—

> "*The Snail: Its Habitat*, &c. Adam Charles. Pschuffer. 21s. 6d.
>
> "There are tender days just before the Spring dares the adventure of the Channel, when our Kentish woods are prescient, as it were, of the South. It is calm . . ."

and so forth, leading gradually up to snails, and bringing in the book here and there about every twentieth line.

When this long article was done, he took it back to the office, and there found the Editor in yet a third mood. He was talking into the telephone, and begged his visitor to wait until he had done. My friend, therefore, took up a copy of the *Spectator*, and attempted to distract his attention with the masterful irony and hard crystalline prose of that paper.

Soon the Editor turned to him and said that Pschuffer's had just let him know by the telephone that they would not advertise after all.

It was now necessary to delete all that there might be upon snails in his article, to head the remainder "My Kentish Home," and to send it immediately to

"*Life in the Open.*" This done, he sat down and wrote upon a scrap of paper in the office the following revised notice, which the Editor glanced at and approved:—

> "*The Snail: Its Habitat*, &c. Adam Charles. Pschuffer. 21s. 6d.
>
> "This work will, perhaps, appeal to specialists. This journal does not profess any capacity of dealing with it, but a glance at its pages is sufficient to show that it would be very ill-suited to ordinary readers. The illustrations are not without merit."

Next morning he was somewhat perturbed to be called up again upon the telephone by the Editor, who spoke to him as follows:—

"I am very sorry, but I have just learnt a most important fact. Adam Charles is standing in our interests at Biggleton. Lord Bailey will be on the platform. You must write a long and favourable review of the book before twelve to-day, and do try and say a little about the author."

He somewhat wearily took up a sheet of paper and wrote what follows:—a passage which I must again recommend to the student as a very admirable specimen of work upon these lines.

> "*The Snail: Its Habitat*, &c. Adam Charles. Pschuffer. 21s. 6d.
>
> "This book comes at a most opportune moment. It is not generally known that Professor Charles was the first to point out the very great importance of the training of the mind in the education of children. It was in May, 1875, that he made this point in the presence of Mr. Gladstone, who was so impressed by the mingled enlightenment and novelty of the view, that he wrote a long and interesting postcard upon the author to a friend of the present writer. Professor Charles may be styled—nay, he

> styles himself—a 'self-made man.' Born in Huddersfield of parents who were weavers in that charming northern city, he was early fascinated by the study of natural science, and was admitted to the Alexandrovna University. . . ."

(And so on, and so on, out of "*Who's Who.*")

> "But this would not suffice for his growing genius."

(And so on, and so on, out of the *Series of Contemporary Agnostics.*)

> " . . . It is sometimes remarkable to men of less wide experience how such spirits find the mere time to achieve their prodigious results. Take, for example, this book on the Snail. . . ."

And he continued in a fine spirit of praise, such as should be given to books of this weight and importance, and to men such as he who had written it. He sent it by boy-messenger to the office.

The messenger had but just left the house when the telephone rang again, and once more it was the Editor, who asked whether the review had been sent off. Knowing how dilatory are the run of journalists, my friend felt some natural pride in replying that he had indeed just despatched the article. The Editor, as luck would have it, was somewhat annoyed by this, and the reason soon appeared when he proceeded to say that the author was another Charles after all, and not the Mr. Charles who was standing for Parliament. He asked whether the original review could still be retained, in which the book, it will be remembered, had been treated with some severity.

My friend permitted himself to give a deep sigh, but was courteous enough to answer as follows:—

"I am afraid it has been destroyed, but I shall be very happy to write another, and I will make it really scathing. You shall have it by twelve."

It was under these circumstances that the review (which many of you must have read) took this final form, which I recommend even more heartily than any of the others to those who may peruse these pages for their profit, as well as for their instruction.

> "*The Snail: Its Habitat,* &c. Adam Charles. Pschuffer. 21s. 6d.
>
> "We desire to have as little to do with this book as possible, and we should recommend some similar attitude to our readers. It professes to be scientific, but the harm books of this kind do is incalculable. It is certainly unfit for ordinary reading, and for our part we will confess that we have not read more than the first few words. They were quite sufficient to confirm the judgment which we have put before our readers, and they would have formed sufficient material for a lengthier treatment had we thought it our duty as Englishmen to dwell further upon the subject."

Let me now turn from the light parenthesis of illuminating anecdote to the sterner part of my task.

We will begin at the beginning, taking the simplest form of review, and tracing the process of production through its various stages.

It is necessary first to procure a few forms, such as are sold by Messrs. Chatsworthy in Chancery Lane, and Messrs. Goldman, of the Haymarket, in which all the skeleton of a review is provided, with blanks left for those portions which must, with the best will in the world, vary according to the book and the author under consideration. There are a large number of these forms, and I would recommend the student who is as yet quite a novice in the trade to select some forty of the most conventional, such as these on page 7 of the catalogue:—

"Mr. ——— has hardly seized the pure beauty of"

"We cannot agree with Mr. ——— in his estimate of"

"Again, how admirable is the following:"

At the same establishments can be procured very complete lists of startling words, which lend individuality and force to the judgment of the Reviewer. Indeed I believe that Mr. Goldman was himself the original patentee of these useful little aids, and among many before me at this moment I would recommend the following to the student:—

"There is somewhat of the	Absolute Immediate Creative Bestial Intense Authoritative Ampitheatrical Lapsed Miggerlish Japhetic Accidental Alkaline Zenotic	in Mr. —'s style." Mrs. —'s Miss —'s

Messrs. Malling, of Duke Street, Soho, sell a particular kind of cartridge paper and some special pins, gum, and a knife, called "The Reviewer's Outfit." I do not know that these are necessary, but they cost only a few pence, and are certainly of advantage in the final process: To wit:—Seizing firmly the book to be reviewed, write down the title, price, publisher, and (in books other than anonymous) the author's name, at the *top* of the sheet of paper you have chosen. The book should then be taken in both hands and opened sharply, with a gesture not easily described, but acquired with very little practice. The test of success is that the book should give a loud crack and lie open of itself upon the table before one. This initial process is technically called "breaking the back" of a book, but we need not trouble ourselves yet with technical terms. One of the pages so disclosed should next be torn out and the word "extract" written in the corner, though not before such sentences have been deleted as will leave the remainder a coherent paragraph. In the case of historical and scientific work, the preface must be torn out bodily, the name of the Reviewer substituted for the word "I," and the whole used as a description of the work in question. What remains is very simple. The forms, extracts, &c., are trimmed, pinned, and gummed in order upon the cartridge paper (in some offices brown paper), and the whole is sent to press.

I need hardly say that only the most elementary form of review can be constructed upon this model, but the simplest notice contains all the factors which enter into the most complicated and most serious of literary criticism and pronouncements.

In this, as in every other practical trade, an ounce of example is worth a ton of precept, and I have much pleasure in laying before the student one of the best examples that has ever appeared in the weekly press of how a careful, subtle, just, and yet tender review, may be written. The complexity of the situation which called it forth, and the lightness of touch required for its successful completion, may be gauged by the fact that Mr. Mayhem was the nephew of my employer, had quarrelled with him at the moment when the notice was written, but will almost certainly be on good terms with him again; he was also, as I privately knew, engaged to the daughter of a publisher who had shares in the works where the review was printed.

A YOUNG POET IN DANGER.

Mr. Mayhem's "Pereant qui Nostra."

We fear that in "Pereant qui Nostra," Mr. Mayhem has hardly added to his reputation, and we might even doubt whether he was well advised to publish it at all. "Tufts in an Orchard" gave such promise, that the author of the exquisite lyrics it contained might easily have rested on the immediate fame that first effort procured him:

> "Lord, look to England; England looks to you,"

and—

> "Great unaffected vampires and the moon,"

are lines the Anglo-Saxon race will not readily let die.

In "Percant qui Nostra," Mr. Mayhem preserves and even increases his old facility of expression, but there is a terrible falling-off in verbal aptitude.

What are we to think of "The greatest general the world has seen" applied as a poetic description to Lord Kitchener? Mr. Mayhem will excuse us if we say that the whole expression is commonplace.

Commonplace thought is bad enough, though it is difficult to avoid when one tackles a great national subject, and thinks what all good patriots and men of sense think also. "Pour être poëte," as M. Yves Guyot proudly said in his receptional address to the French Academy, "Pour être poëte on n'est pas forcément aliéné." But commonplace *language* should always be avoidable, and it is a fault which we cannot but admit we have found throughout Mr. Mayhem's new volume. Thus in "Laura" he compares a young goat to a "tender flower," and in "Billings" he calls some little children "the younglings of the flock." Again, he says of the waves at Dover in a gale that they are "horses all in rank, with manes of snow," and tells us in "Eton College" that the Thames "runs like a silver thread amid the green."

All these similes verge upon the commonplace, even when they do not touch it. However, there is very genuine feeling in the description of his old school, and we have no doubt that the bulk of Etonians will see more in the poem than outsiders can possibly do.

It cannot be denied that Mr. Mayhem has a powerful source of inspiration in his strong patriotism, and the sonnets addressed to Mr. Kruger, Mr. O'Brien, Dr. Clark, and General Mercier are full of vigorous denunciation. It is the more regrettable that he has missed true poetic diction and lost his subtlety in a misapprehension of planes and values.

> "Vile, vile old man, and yet more vile again,"

is a line that we are sure Mr. Mayhem would reconsider in his better moments: "more vile" than what? Than himself? The expression is far too vague.

"Proud Prelate," addressed to General Mercier, must be a misprint, and it is a pity it should have slipped in. What Mr. Mayhem probably meant was "Proud Cæsar" or "soldier," or some other dissyllabic title. The word *prelate* can properly only be applied to a bishop, a mitred abbot, or a vicar apostolic.

"Babbler of Hell, importunate mad fiend, dead canker, crested worm," are vigorous and original, but do not save the sonnet. And as to the last two lines,

> "Nor seek to pierce the viewless shield of years,
> For that you certainly could never do,"

Mr. Mayhem must excuse us if we say that the order of the lines make a sheer bathos.

Perhaps the faults and the excellences of Mr. Mayhem, his fruitful limitations, and his energetic inspirations, can be best appreciated if we quote the following sonnet; the exercise will also afford us the opportunity (which we are sure Mr. Mayhem will not resent in such an old friend) of pointing out the dangers into which his new tendencies may lead him.

> "England, if ever it should be thy fate
> By fortune's turn or accident of chance
> To fall from craven fears of being great,
> And in the tourney with dishevelled lance
> To topple headlong, and incur the Hate
> Of Spain, America, Germany, and France,
> What will you find upon that dreadful date
> To check the backward move of your advance?
>
> A little Glory; purchased not with gold
> Nor yet with Frankincense (the island blood
> Is incommensurate, neither bought nor sold),
> But on the poops where Drake and Nelson stood
> An iron hand, a stern unflinching eye
> To meet the large assaults of Destiny."

Now, here is a composition that not everyone could have written. It is inspired by a vigorous patriotism, it strikes the right note (Mr. Mayhem is a Past Seneschal of the Navy League), and it breathes throughout the motive spirit of our greatest lyrics.

It is the execution that is defective, and it is to execution that Mr. Mayhem must direct himself if he would rise to the level of his own great conceptions.

We will take the sonnet line by line, and make our meaning clear, and we do this earnestly for the sake of a young poet to whom the Anglo-Saxon race owes much, and whom it would be deplorable to see failing, as Kipling appears to be failing, and as Ganzer has failed.

Line 1 is not very striking, but might pass as an introduction; line 2 is sheer pleonasm—after using the word "fate," you cannot use "fortune," "accident," "chance," as though they were amplifications of your first thought. Moreover, the phrase "by *fortune's turn*" has a familiar sound. It is rather an echo than a creation.

In line 3, "craven fears of being great" is taken from Tennyson. The action is legitimate enough. Thus, in Wordsworth's "Excursion" are three lines taken bodily from "Paradise Lost," in Kipling's "Stow it" are whole phrases taken from the *Police Gazette*, and in Mr. Austin's verses you may frequently find portions of a *Standard* leader. Nevertheless, it is a license which a young poet should be chary of. All these others were men of an established reputation before they permitted themselves this liberty.

In line 4, "dishevelled" is a false epithet for "lance"; a lance has no hair; the adjective can only properly be used of a woman, a wild beast, or domestic animal.

In line 5, "incur the hate" is a thoroughly unpoetic phrase—we say so unreservedly. In line 6, we have one of those daring experiments in metre common to our younger poets; therefore we hesitate to pronounce upon it, but (if we may presume to advise) we should give Mr. Mayhem the suggestion made by the *Times* to Tennyson—that he should stick to an exact metre until he felt sure of his style; and in line 8, "the backward move of your advance" seems a little strained.

It is, however, in the sextet that the chief slips of the sonnet appear, and they are so characteristic of the author's later errors, that we cannot but note them; thus, "purchased not with gold or *Frankincense*" is a grievous error. It is indeed a good habit to quote Biblical phrases (a habit which has been the making of half our poets), but not to confuse them: frankincense was never used as coin—even by the Hittites. "Incommensurate" is simply meaningless. How can blood be "incommensurate"? We fear Mr. Mayhem has fallen into the error of polysyllabic effect, a modern pitfall. "Island blood" will, however, stir many a responsive thrill.

The close of the sonnet is a terrible falling off. When you say a thing is purchased, "not with this but——" the reader naturally expects an alternative, instead of which Mr. Mayhem goes right off to another subject! Also (though the allusion to Nelson and Drake is magnificent) the mention of an iron hand and an eye by themselves on a poop seems to us a very violent metaphor.

The last line is bad.

We do not write in this vein to gain any reputation for preciosity, and still less to offend. Mr. Mayhem has many qualities. He has a rare handling of penultimates, much potentiality, large framing; he has a very definite chiaroscuro, and the tones are full and objective; so are the values. We would not restrain a production in which (as a partner in a publishing firm) the present writer is directly interested. But we wish to recall Mr. Mayhem to his earlier and simpler style—to the "Cassowary," and the superb interrupted seventh of "The Altar Ghoul."

England cannot afford to lose that talent.

ON POLITICAL APPEALS.

POLITICAL APPEALS.

It was one of Dr. Caliban's chief characteristics—and perhaps the main source of his power over others—that he could crystallize, or—to use the modern term—"wankle," the thought of his generation into sharp unexpected phrases. Among others, this was constantly upon his lips :—

"*We live in stirring times.*"

If I may presume to add a word to the pronouncements of my revered master, I would re-write the sentence thus :—

"*We live in stirring*—AND CHANGEFUL—*times.*"

It is not only an element of adventure, it is also an element of rapid and unexpected development which marks our period, and which incidentally lends so considerable an influence to genius.

In the older and more settled order, political forces were so well known that no description or analysis of them was necessary: to this day members of our more ancient political families do not read the newspapers. Soon, perhaps, the national life will have entered a new groove, and once more literary gentlemen will but indirectly control the life of the nation.

For the moment, however, their effect is direct and immediate. A vivid prophecy, a strong attack upon

D—2

this statesman or that foreign Government may determine public opinion for a space of over ten days, and matter of this sort is remunerated at the rate of from 15*s*. to 18*s*. 6*d*. per thousand words. When we contrast this with the 9*s*. paid for the translation of foreign classics, the 5*s*. of occasional verse, or even the 10*s*. of police-court reporting, it is sufficiently evident that this kind of composition is the Premier Prose of our time.

There must, indeed, be in London and Manchester, alive at the present moment, at least fifty men who can command the prices I have mentioned, and who, with reasonable industry, can earn as much as £500 a year by their decisions upon political matters. But I should be giving the student very indifferent counsel were I to recommend him for the delivery of his judgment to the beaten track of Leading Articles or to that of specially written and signed communications: the sums paid for such writing never rise beyond a modest level; the position itself is precarious. In London alone, and within a radius of 87 yards from the "Green Dragon," no less than 53 Authors lost their livelihood upon the more respectable papers from an inability to prophecy with any kind of accuracy upon the late war, and this at a time when the majority of regular politicians were able to retain their seats in Parliament and many ministers their rank in the Cabinet.

By far the most durable, the most exalted, and the most effective kind of appeal, is that which is made in a poetic form, especially if that form be vague and symbolic in its character. Nothing is risked and everything is gained by this method, upon which have been founded so many reputations and so many considerable fortunes. The student cannot be too strongly urged to abandon the regular and daily task of set columns—signed or unsigned—for the occasional Flash of Verse if he desire to provoke great wars and to increase his income. It may not always succeed, but the proportion of failures is very small, and at the worst it is but a moment's energy wasted.

"*We are sick*" says one of the most famous among those who have adopted this method, "*We are sick*"—he is speaking not only of himself but of others—"*We are sick for a stave of the song that our fathers sang.*" Turn, therefore, to the dead—who are no longer alive, and with whom no quarrel is to be feared. Make them reappear and lend weight to your contention. Their fame is achieved, and may very possibly support your own. This kind of writing introduces all the elements that most profoundly affect the public: it is mysterious, it is vague, it is authoritative; it is also eminently literary, and I can recall no first-class political appeal of the last fifteen years which has not been cast more or less upon these lines.

The subjects you may choose from are numerous and are daily increasing, but for the amateur the best, without any question, is that of Imperialism. It is a common ground upon which all meet, and upon which every race resident in the wealthier part of London is agreed. Bring forward the great ghosts of the past, let them swell what is now an all but universal chorus. Avoid the more complicated metres, hendecasyllables, and the rest; choose those which neither scan nor rhyme; or, if their subtlety baffles you, fall back upon blank verse, and you should, with the most moderate talent, lay the foundation of a permanent success.

I will append, as is my custom, a model upon which the student may shape his first efforts, though I would not have him copy too faithfully, lest certain idiosyncrasies of manner should betray the plagiarism.

THE IMPERIALIST FEAST.

[*A Hall at the* Grand Oriental. *At a long table are seated innumerable Shades. The walls are decorated with flags of all nations, and a band of musicians in sham uniform are playing very loudly on a daïs.*]

CATULLUS rises and makes a short speech, pointing out the advantages of Strong Men, and making several delicate allusions to Cæsar, who is too much of a gentleman to applaud. He then gives them the toast of "Imperialism," to which there is a hearty response. Lucan replies in a few well-chosen words, and they fall to conversation.

PETRONIUS—I would be crowned with paper flowers
to-night
And scented with the rare opopanax,
Whose savour leads the Orient in, suggesting
The seas beyond Modore.

TALLEYRAND— Shove up, Petronius,
And let me sit as near as possible

To Mr. Bingoe's Grand Imperial Band
With Thirty-seven Brazen Instruments
And Kettle-Drums complete: I hear the players
Discourse the music called "What Ho! She Bumps!"

LORD CHESTERFIELD—What Ho! She Bumps! Likewise! C'est ça! There's 'Air!

LORD GLENALTAMONT OF EPHESUS (*severely*)—Lord Chesterfield! Be worthy of your name.

LORD CHESTERFIELD (*angrily*)—Lord Squab, be worthy of your son-in-law's.

HENRY V.—My Lords! my Lords! What do you with your swords?
I mean, what mean you by this strange demeanour
Which (had you swords and knew you how to use them)
Might . . . . I forget what I was going to say. . . . .
Oh! Yes—— Is this the time for peers to quarrel,
When all the air is thick with Agincourt
And every other night is Crispin's day?
The very supers bellow up and down,
Armed of rude cardboard and wide blades of tin
For England and St. George!

RICHARD YEA AND NAY— You talk too much.
Think more. Revise. Avoid the commonplace;
And when you lack a startling word, invent it.

[*Their quarrel is stopped by* THOMAS JEFFERSON *rising to propose the toast of "The Anglo-Saxon Race."*]

JEFFERSON—If I were asked what was the noblest message

Delivered to the twentieth century,
I should reply—

(Etc., etc. While he maunders on ANTONY, CLEOPATRA, *and* CÆSAR *begin talking rather loud)*

CLEOPATRA—Waiter! I want a little crème de menthe.

(The waiter pays no attention.)

ANTONY—Waiter! A glass of curaçao and brandy.

(Waiter still looks at Jefferson.)

CÆSAR—That is the worst of these contracted dinners.
They give you quite a feed for 3*s*. 6*d*.
And have a splendid Band. I like the Band,
It stuns the soul. . . . . But when you call the waiter
He only sneers and looks the other way.

CLEOPATRA *(makes a moue)*. . . . .

CÆSAR *(archly)*—Was *that* the face that launched a thousand ships
And sacked . . . .

ANTONY *(angrily)*—Oh! Egypt! Egypt! Egypt!

THOMAS JEFFERSON *(ending, interrupts the quarrel)*.
. . . . blessings
Of order, cleanliness, and business methods.
The base of Empire is a living wage.
One King . . . . *(applause)* . . . . *(applause)*
. . . . *(applause)* shall always wave
. . . . *(applause)*
. . . . *(loud applause)* . . . . *(applause)*
THE REIGN OF LAW!

(Thunders of applause)

NAPOLEON (*rising to reply*)—I am myself a strong Imperialist.

A *brochure*, very recently compiled
(Which, pardon me, I do not mean to read),
Neglects the point, I think; the Anglo-Saxon
. . . . (&c. &c.)

GEORGE III. (*to Burke*)—Who's that? Eh, what? Who's that? Who ever's that?

BURKE—Dread sire! It is the Corsican Vampire.

GEORGE III.—Napoleon? What? I thought that he was leaner.
I thought that he was leaner. What? What? What?

NAPOLEON (*sitting down*) . . . . such dispositions! Order! *Tête d'Armée!*

(*Slight applause*)

HEROD (*rises suddenly without being asked, crosses his arms, glares, and shouts very loudly*).

Ha! Would you have Imperial hearing? Hounds!
I am that Herod which is he that am
The lonely Lebanonian (*interruption*) who despaired
In Deep Marsupial Dens . . . . (*cries of "Sit down!"*)
. . . . In dreadful hollows
To—("*Sit down!*")—tear great trees with the teeth, and hurricanes—("*Sit down!*")—
That shook the hills of Moab!

CHORUS OF DEAD MEN—Oh! Sit down.

(*He is swamped by the clamour, in the midst of which Lucullus murmurs to himself*)

LUCULLUS (*musing*)—The banquet's done. There was
a tribute drawn
Of anchovies and olives and of soup
In tins of conquered nations; subject whiting:
Saddle of mutton from the antipodes
Close on the walls of ice; Laponian pheasants;
Eggs of Canadian rebels, humbled now
To such obeisance—scrambled eggs—and butter
From Brittany enslaved, and the white bread
Hardened for heroes in the test of time,
Was California's offering. But the cheese,
The cheese was ours. . . . . Oh! but the
glory faded
Of feasting at repletion mocks our arms
And threatens even Empire.

(*Great noise of Vulgarians, a mob of people, heralds, trumpets, flags. Enter* VITELLIUS.)

VITELLIUS— I have dined!
But not with you. The master of the world
Has dined alone and at his own expense.
And oh!—I am almost too full for words—
But oh! My lieges, I have used you well!
I have commanded fifteen hundred seats
And standing room for something like a thousand
To view my triumph over Nobody
Upon the limelit stage.

HEROD— Oh! rare Vitellius,
Oh! Prominent great Imperial ears! Oh! Mouth
To bellow largesse! Oh! And rolling Thunder,
And trains of smoke. And oh! . .

VITELLIUS— Let in the vulgar

To see the master sight of their dull lives:
Great Cæsar putting on his overcoat.
And then, my loved companions, we'll away
To see the real Herod in the Play.

(*The Shades pass out in a crowd. In the street* THEOCRITUS *is heard singing in a voice that gets fainter and fainter with distance.* . . . .)

"Put me somewhere ea-heast of Su-hez,
W'ere the best is loi-hoike the worst—
W'ere there hain' no"—(*and so forth*).

FINIS.

It is not enough to compose such appeals as may quicken the nation to a perception of her peculiar mission; it is necessary to paint for her guidance the abominations and weakness of foreign countries. The young writer may be trusted to know his duty instinctively in this matter, but should his moral perception be blunted, a sharper argument will soon remind him of what he owes to the Common Conscience of Christians. He that cannot write, and write with zeal, upon the Balkans, or upon Finland, or upon the Clerical trouble, or upon whatever lies before us to do for righteousness, is not worthy of a place in English letters: the public and his editor will very soon convince him of what he has lost by an unmanly reticence.

His comrades, who are content to deal with such matters as they arise, will not be paid at a higher rate: but they will be paid more often. They will not infrequently be paid from several sources; they will have many opportunities for judging those financial questions which are invariably mixed up with the great battle against the Ultramontane, the Cossack and the Turk. In Cairo, Frankfort, Pretoria, Mayfair, Shanghai, their latter days confirm Dr. Caliban's profound conclusion: "Whosoever works for Humanity works, whether he know it or not, for himself as well."*

I earnestly beseech the reader of this text-book, especially if he be young, to allow no false shame to modify his zeal in judging the vileness of the Continent. We know whatever can be known; all criticism or qualification is hypocrisy; all silence is cowardice. There is work to be done. Let the writer take up his pen and *write*.

I had some little hesitation what model to put before the student. This book does not profess to be more than an introduction to the elements of our science; I therefore omitted what had first seemed to me of some value, the letters written on a special commission to Pondicherry during the plague and famine in that unhappy and ill-governed remnant of a falling empire. The articles on the tortures in the Phillipines were never printed, and might mislead. I have preferred to show Priestcraft and Liberty in their eternal struggle as they appeared to me in the character of Special Commissioner for *Out and About* during the troubles of 1901. It is clear, and I think unbiassed; it opens indeed in that light fashion which is a concession to contemporary journalism: but the half-

* This Phrase closes the XXXIVth of Dr. Caliban's "Subjects for Sinners."

frivolous exterior conceals a permanent missionary purpose. Its carefully collected array of facts give, I suggest, a vivid picture of one particular battlefield; that whereon there rage to-day the opposed forces which will destroy or save the French people. The beginner could not have a better introduction to his struggle against the infamies of Clericalism. Let him ask himself (as Mr. Gardy, M.P., asked in a letter to *Out and About*) the indignant question, "Could such things happen here in England?"

THE SHRINE OF ST. LOUP.

My excellent good Dreyfusards, anti-Dreyfusards, Baptists, Anabaptists, pre-Monstratentians, antiquaries, sterling fellows, foreign correspondents, home-readers, historians, Nestorians, philosophers, Deductionists, Inductionists, Prætorians (I forgot those), Cæsarists, Lazarists, Catholics, Protestants, Agnostics and militant atheists, as also all you Churchmen, Nonconformists, Particularists, very strong secularists, and even you, my well-beloved little brethren called The Peculiar People, give ear attentively and listen to what is to follow, and you shall learn more of a matter that has wofully disturbed you than ever you would get from the *Daily Mail* or from Mynheer van Damm, or even from Dr. Biggles' *Walks and Talks in France.*

In an upper valley of the Dauphiné there is a village called Lagarde. From this village, at about half-past four o'clock of a pleasant June morning, there walked out with his herd one Jean Rigors, a herdsman and half-wit. He had not proceeded very far towards the pastures above the village, and the sun was barely showing above the peak profanely called The Three Bishops, when he had the fortune to meet the Blessed St. Loup, or Lupus, formerly a hermit in that valley, who had died some fourteen hundred years ago, but whose name, astonishing as it may seem to the author of *The Justification of Fame*, is still remembered among the populace. The Blessed Lupus admonished the peasant, recalling the neglect into which public worship had fallen, reluctantly promised a sign whereby it might be re-created among the faithful, and pointed out a nasty stream of muddy water, one out of fifty that trickled from the moss of the Alps. He then struck M. Rigors a slight, or, as some accounts have it, a heavy, blow with his staff, and disappeared in glory.

Jean Rigors, who could not read or write, being a man over thirty, and having therefore forgotten the excellent free lessons provided by the Republic in primary schools, was not a little astonished at the apparition. Having a care to tether a certain calf whom he knew to be light-headed, he left the rest of the herd to its own unerring instincts, and ran back to the village to inform the parish priest of the very remarkable occurrence of which he had been the witness or victim. He found upon his return that the morning Mass, from which he had been absent off and on for some seven years, was already at the Gospel, and attended to it with quite singular devotion, until in the space of some seventeen minutes he was able to meet the priest in the sacristy and inform him of what had happened.

The priest, who had heard of such miraculous appearances in other villages, but (being a humble man, unfitted for worldly success and idiotic in business matters) had never dared to hope that one would be vouchsafed to his own cure, proceeded at once to the source of the muddy streamlet, and (unhistorical as the detail may seem to the author of *Our Old Europe, Whence and Whither?*) neglected to reward the hind, who, indeed, did not expect pecuniary remuneration, for these two excellent reasons:—First, that he knew the priest to be by far the poorest man in the parish; secondly, that he thought a revelation from the other world incommensurate with money payments even to the extent of a five-franc piece. The next Sunday (that is, three days afterwards) the priest, who had previously informed his brethren throughout the Canton, preached a sermon upon the decay of religion and the growing agnosticism of the modern world—a theme which, as they had heard it publicly since the Christian religion had been established by Constantine in those parts and privately for one hundred and twenty-five years before, his congregation received with some legitimate languor. When, however, he came to what was the very gist of his remarks, the benighted foreigners pricked up their ears (a physical atavism impossible to our own more enlightened community), and Le Sieur Rigors, who could still remember the greater part of the services of the Church, was filled with a mixture of nervousness and pride, while the good priest informed his hearers, in language that would have been eloquent had he not been trained in the little seminary, that the great St. Lupus himself had appeared to a devout member of his parish and had pointed out to him a miraculous spring, for the proper enshrinement of which he requested—nay, he demanded—the contributions of the faithful.

At that one sitting the excellent hierarch received no less a sum than 1053 francs and 67 centimes; the odd two-centimes (a coin that has disappeared from the greater part of France) being contributed by a road-mender, who was well paid by the State, but who was in the custom of receiving charity from tourists; the said tourists being under the erroneous impression that he was a beggar. He also, by the way, would entertain the more Anglo-Saxon of these with the folk-lore of the district, in which his fertile imagination was never at fault.

It will seem astonishing to the author of *Village Communities in Western Europe* to hear of so large a sum as £40 being subscribed by the congregation of this remote village, and it would seem still more astonishing to him could he see the very large chapel erected over the spring of St. Loup. I do not say that he would understand the phenomenon, but I do say that he would become a more perturbed and therefore a wiser man did he know the following four facts:—(1) That the freehold value of the village and its communal land, amounting to the sum of a poor £20,000, was not in the possession of a landlord, but in that of these wretched peasants. (2) That the one rich man of the neighbourhood, a retired glove-maker, being also a fanatic, presented his subscriptions in such a manner that they were never heard of. He had, moreover, an abhorrence for the regulation of charity. (3) That the master mason in the neighbouring town had in his youth been guilty of several mortal sins, and was so weak as to imagine that a special tender would in such a case make a kind of reparation; and (4) that the labourers employed were too ignorant to cheat and too illiterate to combine.

The new shrine waxed and prospered exceedingly, and on the Thursday following its dedication an epileptic, having made use of the water, was restored to a normal, and even commonplace, state of mind. On the Friday a girl, who said that she had been haunted by devils (though until then no one had heard of the matter), declared, upon drinking a cup from the spring of St. Loup, that she was now haunted by angels—a very much pleasanter condition of affairs. The Sunday following, the village usurer, who called himself Bertollin, but who was known to be a wicked foreigner from beyond the Alps, of the true name of Bertolino, ran into the inn like one demented, and threw down the total of his ill-gotten gains for the benefit of the shrine. They amounted, indeed, to but a hundred francs, but then his clientèle were close and skin-flint, as peasant proprietors and free men generally are the world over; and it was well known that the cobbler, who had himself borrowed a small sum for a month, and quadrupled it in setting up lodgings for artists, had been unable to recover from the usurer the mending of his boots.

By this time the Bishop had got wind of the new shrine, and wrote to the Curé of Lagarde a very strong letter, in which, after reciting the terms of the Concordat, Clause 714 of the Constitution and the decree of May 29th, 1854, he pointed out that by all these and other fundamental or organic laws of the Republic, he was master in his own diocese. He rebuked the curé for the superstitious practice which had crept into his cure, ordered the chapel to be used for none but ordinary purposes, and issued a pastoral letter upon the evils of local superstitions. This pastoral letter was read with unction and holy mirth in the neighbouring monastery of Bernion (founded in defiance of the law by the widow of a President of the Republic), but with sorrow and without comment in the little church of Lagarde.

The Minister of the Interior and the Minister of Public Worship, each in his separate way, proceeded to stamp out this survival of the barbaric period of Europe. The first by telling the Prefect to tell the sub-Prefect to tell the Mayor that any attempt to levy taxes in favour of the shrine would be administratively punished: the second by writing a sharp official note to the Bishop for not having acted on the very day that St. Loup appeared to the benighted herdsman. The sub-Prefect came from the horrible town of La Rochegayere and lunched with the Mayor, who was the donor of the new stained-glass window in the church, and they talked about the advantages of forcing the Government to construct a road through the valley to accommodate the now numerous pilgrims; a subject which the sub-Prefect, who was about to be promoted, approached with official nonchalance, but the Mayor (who owned the principal inn) with pertinacity and fervour. They then went out, the Mayor in his tricolour scarf to lock up the gate in front of the holy well, the sub-Prefect to escort his young wife to the presbytery, where she left a gift of 500 francs: the sub-Prefect thought it improper for a lady to walk alone.

Upon the closure of the shrine a local paper (joint property of the Bishop and a railway contractor) attacked the atheism of the Government. A local duchess, who was ignorant of the very terminology of religion, sent a donation of five thousand francs to the curé; with this the excellent man built a fine approach to the new chapel, "which," as he sorrowfully and justly observed, "the faithful may approach, though an atheistic Government forbids the use of the shrine." That same week, by an astonishing accident, the Ministry was overturned; the Minister of the Interior was compelled to retire into private life, and lived dependent upon his uncle (a Canon of Rheims). The Minister of Public Worship (who had become increasingly unpopular through the growth of anti-Semitic feeling) took up his father's money-lending business at Antwerp.

Next week the lock and seals were discovered to have been in some inexplicable way removed from the gate of the well and (by Article 893 of the Administrative Code) before they could be replaced an action was necessary at the assize-town of Grenoble. This action (by the Order of 1875 on Law Terms) could not take place for six months; and in that interval an astonishing number of things happened at Lagarde.

An old Sapper General, who had devised the special obturator for light quick-firing guns, and who was attached to the most backward superstitions, came in full uniform to the Chapel and gave the shrine 10,000 francs: a mysteriously large endowment, as this sum was nearly half his income, and he had suffered imprisonment in youth for his Republican opinions. He said it was for the good of his soul, but the editor of the *Horreur* knew better, and denounced him. He was promptly retired upon a pension about a third greater than that to which he was legally entitled, and received by special secret messenger from the Minister of War an earnest request to furnish a memorandum on the fortifications of the Isère and to consider himself inspector, upon mobilisation, of that important line of defence.

Two monks, who had walked all the way from Spain, settled in a house near the well. A pilgrim, who had also evidently come from a prodigious distance on foot, but gave false information as to his movements, was arrested by the police and subsequently released. The arrest was telegraphed to the *Times* and much commented upon, but the suicide of a prominent London solicitor and other important news prevented any mention of his release.

A writer of great eminence, who had been a leading sceptic all his life, stayed at Lagarde for a month and became a raving devotee. His publishers (MM. Hermann Khan) punished him by refusing to receive his book upon the subject; but by some occult influence, probably that of the Jesuits, he was paid several hundreds for it by the firm of Zadoc et Cie; ten years afterwards he died of a congested liver, a catastrophe which some ascribed to a Jewish plot, and others treated as a proof that his intellect had long been failing.

A common peasant fellow, that had been paralysed for ten years, bathed in the water and walked away in a sprightly fashion afterwards. This was very likely due to his ignorance, for a doctor who narrowly watched the whole business has proved that he did not know the simplest rudiments of arithmetic or history, and how should such a fellow understand so difficult a disease as paralysis of the Taric nerve—especially if it were (as the doctor thought quite evident) complicated by a stricture of the Upper Dalmoid?

Two deaf women were, as is very commonly the case with enthusiasts of this kind, restored to their hearing; for how long we do not know, as their subsequent history was not traced for more than five years.

A dumb boy talked, but in a very broken fashion, and as he had a brother a priest and another brother in the army, trickery was suspected.

An English merchant, who had some trouble with

his eyes, bathed in the water at the instance of a sister who desired to convert him. He could soon see so well that he was able to write to the *Freethinker* an account of his healing, called "The Medicinal Springs of Lagarde," but, as he has subsequently gone totally blind, the momentary repute against ophthalmia which the water might have obtained was nipped in the bud.

What was most extraordinary of all, a very respectable director of a railway came to the village quietly, under an assumed name, and, after drinking the water, made a public confession of the most incredible kind and has since become a monk. His son, to whom he made over his whole fortune, had previously instituted a demand at law to be made guardian of his estates; but, on hearing of his father's determination to embrace religion, he was too tolerant to pursue the matter further.

To cut a long story short, as Homer said when he abruptly closed the *Odyssey*, some 740 cases of miraculous cures occurred between the mysterious opening of the gates and the date for the trial at Grenoble. In that period a second and much larger series of buildings had begun to arise; the total property involved in the case amounted to 750,000 francs, and (by clause 61 of the Regulation on Civil Tribunals) the local court of assize was no longer competent. Before, however, the case could be removed to Paris, the assent of the Grenoble bench had to be formally obtained, and this, by the singularly Republican rule of "*Non-avant*" (instituted by Louis XI.), took just two years. By that time the new buildings were finished, eight priests were attached to the Church, a monastery of seventy-two monks, five hotels, a golf links, and a club were in existence. The total taxes paid by Lagarde to the Treasury amounted to half-a-million francs a year.

The Government had become willing (under the "Compromise of '49," which concerns Departments *v.* the State in the matter of internal communications) to build a fine, great road up to Lagarde. There was also a railway, a Custom House, and a project of sub-prefecture. Moreover, in some underhand way or other, several hundred people a month were cured of various ailments, from the purely subjective (such as buzzing in the ears) to those verging upon the truly objective (such as fracture of the knee-pan or the loss of an eye).

The Government is that of a practical and common-sense people. It will guide or protect, but it cannot pretend to coerce. Lagarde therefore flourishes, the Bishop is venerated, the monastery grumbles in silence, and there is some talk of an Hungarian journalist, born in Constantinople, whose father did time for cheating in the Russian Army, writing one of his fascinating anti-religious romances in nine hundred pages upon the subject. You will learn far more from such a book than you can possibly learn from the narrow limits of the above.

THE SHORT STORY.

THE short story is the simplest of all forms of literary composition. It is at the same time by far the most lucrative. It has become (to use one of Dr. Caliban's most striking phrases) "part of the atmosphere of our lives." In a modified form, it permeates our private correspondence, our late Baron Reuter's telegraphic messages, the replies of our cabinet ministers, the rulings of our judges; and it has become inseparable from affirmations upon oath before Magistrates, Registrars, Coroners, Courts of Common Jurisdiction, Official Receivers, and all others qualified under 17 Vic. 21, Caps. 2 and 14; sub-section III.

To return to the short story. Its very reason for being (*raison d'être*) is simplicity. It suits our strenuous, active race; nor would I waste the student's time by recalling the fact that, in the stagnant civilization of China, a novel or play deals with the whole of the hero's life, in its minutest details, through seventy years. The contrast conveys an awful lesson!

Let us confine ourselves, however, to the purpose of these lines, and consider the short story; for it is the business of every true man to do what lies straight before him as honestly and directly as he can.

The Short Story, on account of its simplicity, coupled with the high rates of pay attached to it, attracts at the outset the great mass of writers. Several are successful, and in their eager rapture (I have but to mention John and Mary Hitherspoon) produce such numerous examples of this form of art, that the student may ask what more I have to teach him? In presenting a model for his guidance, and reproducing the great skeleton lines upon which the Short Story is built up, I would remind my reader that it is my function to instruct and his to learn; and I would warn him that even in so elementary a branch of letters as is this, "pride will have a fall."

It is not necessary to dwell further upon this unpleasant aspect of my duty.

Let us first consider where the writer of the Short Story stands before the Law. What is her Legal Position as to (*a*) the length, (*b*) the plot of a short story which she may have contracted to deliver on a certain date to a particular publisher, editor, agent, or creditor? The following two decisions apply:—

Mabworthy v. Crawley. *Mabworthy v. Crawley.*—Mrs. Mabworthy brought an action against Crawley & Co. to recover payment due for a short story ordered of her by defendant. Defendant pleaded lack of specific performance, as story dealt with gradual change of spiritual outlook, during forty years, of maiden lady inhabiting Ealing. It was held by Mr. Justice Pake that the subject so treated was not of "ordinary length." Judgment for the defendant. Mrs. Mabworthy, prompted by her sex, fortune, and solicitor to appeal, the matter was brought before the Court of Appeal, which decided that the word "ordinary" was equivalent to the word "reasonable." Judgment for the defendant, with costs. Mrs. Mabworthy, at the instigation of the Devil, sold a reversion and carried the matter to the House of Lords, where it was laid down that "a Short Story should be of such length as would be found tolerable by any man of ordinary firmness and courage." Judgment for the defendant.

The next case is the case of—

Gibson v. Acle. *Gibson v. Acle.*—In this case, Mr. Phillip Gibson, the well-known publisher, brought an action for the recovery of a sum of £3. 10*s*., advanced to Miss Acle, of "The Wolfcote," Croydon, in consideration of her contracting to supply a short story, with regard to the manuscript of which he maintained, upon receiving it, that (1) it was not a story, and (2) it was not technically "short," as it filled but eighteen lines in the very large type known as grand pica. Three very important points were decided in this case; for the Judge (Mr.

Justice Veale, brother of Lord Burpham) maintained, with sturdy common sense, that if a publisher bought a manuscript, no matter what, so long as it did not offend common morals or the public security of the realm, he was bound to "print, comfort, cherish, defend, enforce, push, maintain, advertize, circulate, and make public the same"; and he was supported in the Court of Crown Cases Reserved in his decision that:

First: the word "short" was plainly the more applicable the less lengthy were the matter delivered: and

Secondly: the word "story" would hold as a definition for any concoction of words whatsoever, of which it could be proved that it was built up of separate sentences, such sentences each to consist of at least one predicate and one verb, real or imaginary.

Both these decisions are quite recent, and may be regarded as the present state of the law on the matter.

Once the legal position of the author is grasped, it is necessary to acquire the five simple rules which govern the Short Story.

1st. It should, as a practical matter apart from the law, contain some incident.

2nd. That incident should take place on the sea, or in brackish, or at least tidal, waters.

3rd. The hero should be English-speaking, white or black.

4th. His adventures should be horrible; but no kind of moral should be drawn from them, unless it be desired to exalt the patriotism of the reader.

5th. Every short story should be divided by a "Cæsura": that is, it should break off sharp in the middle, and you have then the choice of three distinct courses:

(*a*.) To stop altogether—as is often done by people who die, and whose remains are published.

(*b*). To go on with a totally different subject. This method is not to be commended to the beginner. It is common to rich or popular writers; and even they have commonly the decency to put in asterisks.

(*c*). To go on with your story where it left off, as I have done in the model which follows.

That model was constructed especially with the view to guide the beginner. Its hero is a fellow subject, white—indeed, an Englishman. The scene is laid in water, not perhaps salt, but at least brackish. The adventure preys upon the mind. The moral is doubtful: the Cæsura marked and obvious. Moreover, it begins in the middle, which (as I omitted to state above) is the very hall-mark of the Vivid Manner.

THE ACCIDENT TO MR. THORPE.

WHEN Mr. Thorpe, drysalter, of St. Mary Axe, E.C., fell into the water, it was the opinion of those who knew him best that he would be drowned. I say "those who knew him best" because, in the crowd that immediately gathered upon the embankment, there were present not a few of his friends. They had been walking home together on this fine evening along the river side, and now that Mr. Thorpe was in such peril, not one could be got to do more than lean upon the parapet shouting for the police, though they should have known how useless was that body of men in any other than its native element. Alas! how frail a thing is human friendship, and how terribly does misfortune bring it to the test.

How had Mr. Thorpe fallen into the water? I am not surprised at your asking that question. It argues a very observant, critical, and accurate mind; a love of truth; a habit of weighing evidence; and altogether a robust, sturdy, practical, Anglo-Saxon kind of an attitude, that does you credit. You will not take things on hearsay, and there is no monkish credulity about you. I congratulate you. You say (and rightly) that Honest Merchants do not fall into the Thames for nothing, the thing is unusual; you want (very properly) to know how it happened, or, as you call it, "occurred." I cannot tell you. I was not there at the time. All I know is, that he did fall in, and that, as matter of plain fact (and you are there to judge fact, remember, not law), Mr. Thorpe was at 6.15 in the evening of June 7th, 1892, floundering about in the water a little above Cleopatra's Needle; and there are a cloud of witnesses.

It now behoves me to detail with great accuracy the circumstances surrounding his immersion, the degree of danger that he ran, and how he was saved.

In the first place, Mr. Thorpe fell in at the last of the ebb, so that there was no tide to sweep him out to sea; in the second place, the depth of water at that spot was exactly five feet two inches, so that he could—had he but known it—have walked ashore (for he was, of course, over six feet in height); in the third place, the river has here a good gravelly bed, as you ought to know, for the clay doesn't begin till you get beyond Battersea Bridge—and, by the way, this gravel accounts for the otherwise inexplicable phenomenon of the little boys that will dive for pennies at low tide opposite the shot tower; in the fourth place, the water, as one might have imagined at that season of the year, was warm and comfortable; in the fifth place, there lay but a few yards from him a Police Pier, crowded with lines, lifebuoys, boats, cork-jackets, and what not, and decorated, as to its Main Room, with a large placard entitled "First help to the drowning," the same being illustrated with cuts, showing a man of commonplace features fallen into the hands of his religious opponents and undergoing the torture. Therefore it is easy to see that he could have either saved himself or have been saved by others without difficulty. Indeed, for Mr. Thorpe to have drowned, it would have been necessary for him to have exercised the most determined self-control, and to have thought out the most elaborate of suicidal plans; and, as a fact, he was within forty-three seconds of his falling in pulled out again by a boat-hook, which was passed through the back of his frock coat: and that is a lesson in favour of keeping one's coat buttoned up like a gentleman, and not letting it flap open like an artist or an anarchist, or a fellow that writes for the papers. But I digress. The point is, that Mr. Thorpe was immediately saved, and there (you might think) was an end of the matter. Indeed, the thing seems to come to a conclusion of its own, and to be a kind of epic, for it has a beginning where Mr. Thorpe falls into the water (and, note you, the beginning of all epics is, or should be, out of the text); it has a middle or "action," where Mr. Thorpe is floundering about like a sea monster, and an end, where he is pulled out again. They are of larger scope than this little story, and written in a pompous manner, yet the *Iliad*, the *Æneid*, Abbo's *Siege of Paris*, the *Chanson de Roland*, *Orlando Furioso*, *Thalaba the Destroyer*, and Mr. Davidson's shorter lyrics have no better claim to be epics in their essentials than has this relation of *The Accident to Mr. Thorpe*. So, then (you say), that is the end; thank you for the story; we are much obliged. If ever you have another simple little story to tell, pray publish it at large, and do not keep if for the exquisite delight of your private circle. We thank you again a thousand times. Good morrow.

Softly, softly. I beg that there may be no undue haste or sharp conclusions; there is something more to come. Sit you down and listen patiently. Was there ever an epic that was not continued? Did not the Rhapsodists of Cos piece together the *Odyssey* after their successful *Iliad?* Did not Dionysius Paracelsus write a tail to the *Æneid?* Was not the *Chanson de Roland* followed by the *Four Sons of Aymon?* Could Southey have been content with Thalaba had he not proceeded to write the adventures in America of William ap Williams, or some other Welshman whose name I forget? Eh? Well, in precisely the same manner, I propose to add a second and completing narrative to this of Mr. Thorpe's accident; so let us have no grumbling.

And to understand what kind of thing followed his fall into the water, I must explain to you that nothing had ever happened to Mr. Thorpe before; he had never sailed a boat, never ridden a horse, never had a fight, never written a book, never climbed a mountain—indeed, I might have set out in a long litany, covering several pages, the startling, adventurous, and dare-devil things that Mr. Thorpe had never done; and were I to space out my work so, I should be well in the fashion, for does not the immortal Kipling (who is paid by the line) repeat his own lines half-a-dozen times over, and use in profusion the lines of well-known ballads? He does; and so have I therefore the right to space and stretch my work in whatever fashion will spin out the space most fully; and if I do not do so, it is because I am as eager as you can possibly be to get to the end of this chronicle.

Well then, nothing had ever happened to Mr. Thorpe before, and what was the result? Why that this aqueous adventure of his began to grow and possess him as you and I are possessed by our more important feats, by our different distant journeys, our bold speculations, our meeting with grand acquaintances, our outwitting of the law; and I am sorry to say that Mr. Thorpe in a very short time began to lie prodigiously. The symptoms of this perversion first appeared a few days after the accident, at a lunch which he attended (with the other directors of the Marine Glue Company) in the City. The company was in process of negotiating a very difficult piece of business, that required all the attention of the directors, and, as is usual under such circumstances, they fell to telling amusing tales to one another. One of them had just finished his story of how a nephew of his narrowly escaped lynching at Leadville, Colorado, when Mr. Thorpe, who had been making ponderous jokes all the morning, was suddenly observed to grow thoughtful, and (after first ascertaining with some care that there was no one present who had seen him fall in) he astonished the company by saying: "I cannot hear of such escapes from death without awe. It was but the other day that I was saved as by a miracle from drowning." Then he added, after a little pause, "My whole life seemed to pass before me in a moment."

Now this was not true. Mr. Thorpe's mind at the moment he referred to had been wholly engrossed by the peculiar sensation that follows the drinking of a gallon of water suddenly when one is not in the least thirsty; but he had already told the tale so often, that he was fully persuaded of it, and, by this time, believed that his excellent and uneventful life had been presented to him as it is to the drowning people in books.

His fall was rapid. He grew in some vague way to associate his adventure with the perils of the sea. Whenever he crossed the Channel he would draw some fellow passenger into a conversation, and, having cunningly led it on to the subject of shipwreck, would describe the awful agony of battling with the waves, and the outburst of relief on being saved. At first he did not actually say that he had himself struggled in the vast and shoreless seas of the world, but bit by bit the last shreds of accuracy left him, and he took to painting with minute detail in his conversations the various scenes of his danger and salvation. Sometimes it was in the "steep water off the Banks;" sometimes in "the glassy steaming seas and on the feverish coast of the Bight;" sometimes it was "a point or two norr'ard of the Owers light"—but it was always terrible, graphic, and a lie.

This habit, as it became his unique preoccupation, cost him not a little. He lost his old friends who had seen his slight adventure, and he wasted much time in spinning these yarns, and much money in buying books of derring-do and wild 'scapes at sea. He loved those who believed his stories to be true, and shocked the rare minds that seemed to catch in them a suspicion of exaggeration. He could not long frequent the same society, and he strained his mind a little out of shape by the perpetual necessity of creative effort. None the less, I think that, on the whole, he gained. It made him an artist: he saw great visions of heaving waters at night; he really had, in fancy, faced death in a terrible form, and this gave him a singular courage in his last moments. He said to the doctor, with a slight calm smile, "Tell me the worst; I have been through things far more terrifying than this;" and when he was offered consolation by his weeping friends, he told them that "no petty phrases of ritual devotion were needed to soothe a man who had been face to face with Nature in her wildest moods." So he died, comforted by his illusion, and for some days after the funeral his sister would hold him up to his only and favourite nephew as an example of a high and strenuous life lived with courage, and ended in heroic quiet. Then they all went to hear the will read.

But the will was the greatest surprise of all. For it opened with these words:—

> "Having some experience of the perils they suffer that go down to the sea in ships, and of the blessedness of unexpected relief and rescue, I, John Curtall Thorpe, humbly and gratefully reminiscent of my own wonderful and miraculous snatching from the jaws of death . . ."

And it went on to leave the whole property (including the little place in Surrey), in all (after Sir William Vernon Harcourt's death duties had been paid) some £69,337. 6*s*. 3*d*. to the Lifeboat Fund, which badly needed it. Nor was there any modifying codicil but one, whereby the sum of £1000, free of duty, was left to Sylvester Sarassin, a poetic and long-haired young man, who had for years attended to his tales with reverent attention, and who had, indeed, drawn up, or "Englished" (as he called it), the remarkable will of the testator.

Many other things that followed this, the law-suit, the quarrel of the nephew with Sarassin, and so forth, I would relate had I the space or you the patience. But it grows late; the oil in the bulb is exhausted. The stars, which (in the beautiful words of Theocritus) "tremble and always follow the quiet wheels of the night," warn me that it is morning. Farewell.

THE SHORT LYRIC.

MANY Guides to Literature give no rules for the manufacture of short lyrics, and nearly all of them omit to furnish the student with an example of this kind of composition.

The cause of this unfortunate neglect (as I deem it) is not far to seek. Indeed in one Text Book (Mrs. Railston's *Book for Beginners*. Patteson. 12*s*. 6*d*.) it is set down in so many words. "The Short Lyric," says Mrs. Railston in her preface, "is practically innocent of pecuniary value. Its construction should be regarded as a pastime rather than as serious exercise; and even for the purposes of recreation, its fabrication is more suited to the leisure of a monied old age than to the struggle of eager youth, or the full energies of a strenuous manhood" (p. xxxiv.).

The judgment here pronounced is surely erroneous. The short Lyric is indeed not very saleable (though there are exceptions even to that rule—the first Lord Tennyson is said to have received £200 for *The Throstle*); it is (I say) not very saleable, but it is of great indirect value to the writer, especially in early youth. A reputation can be based upon a book of short lyrics which will in time procure for its author Reviewing work upon several newspapers, and sometimes, towards his fortieth year, the editorship of a magazine; later in life it will often lead to a pension, to the command of an army corps, or even to the governorship of a colony.

I feel, therefore, no hesitation in describing at some length the full process of its production, or in presenting to the student a careful plan of the difficulties which will meet him at the outset.

To form a proper appreciation of these last, it is necessary to grasp the fundamental fact that they all proceed from the inability of busy editors and readers to judge the quality of verse; hence the rebuffs and delays that so often overcast the glorious morning of the Poetic Soul.

At the risk of some tedium—for the full story is of considerable length—I will show what is their nature and effect, in the shape of a relation of what happened to Mr. Peter Gurney some years ago, before he became famous.

Mr. Peter Gurney (I may say it without boasting) is one of my most intimate friends. He is, perhaps, the most brilliant of that brilliant group of young poets which includes Mr. John Stewart, Mr. Henry Hawk, &c., and which is known as the "Cobbley school," from the fact that their historic meeting-ground was the house of Mr. Thomas Cobbley, himself no mean poet, but especially a creative, seminal critic, and uncle of Mr. Gurney. But to my example and lesson:—

Mr. Gurney was living in those days in Bloomsbury, and was occupied in reading for the bar.

He was by nature slothful and unready, as is indeed the sad habit of literary genius; he rose late, slept long, eat heartily, drank deeply, read newspapers, began things he never finished, and wrote the ending of things whose beginnings he never accomplished; in a word, he was in every respect the man of letters. He looked back continually at the stuff he had written quite a short time before, and it always made him hesitate in his opinion of what he was actually engaged in. It was but six months before the events herein set down that he had written—

"The keep of the unconquerable mind"—

only to discover that it was clap-trap and stolen from Wordsworth at that. How, then, could he dare send off the sonnet—

"If all intent of unsubstantial art"—

and perhaps get it printed in the *Nineteenth Century* or the *North American Review*, when (for all he knew) it might really be very poor verse indeed?

These two things, then, his sloth and his hesitation in criticism, prevented Peter from sending out as much as he should have done. But one fine day of last summer, a kind of music passed into him from universal nature, and he sat down and wrote these remarkable lines:—

"He is not dead; the leaders do not die,
But rather, lapt in immemorial ease
Of merit consummate, they passing, stand;
And rapt from rude reality, remain;
And in the flux and eddy of time, are still.
Therefore I call it consecrated sand
Wherein they left their prints, nor overgrieve;
An heir of English earth let English earth receive."

He had heard that *Culture* of Boston, Mass., U.S.A., paid more for verse than any other review, so he sent it off to that address, accompanied by a very earnest little letter, calling the gem "Immortality," and waiting for the answer.

The editor of *Culture* is a businesslike man, who reads his English mail on the quay at New York, and takes stamped envelopes and rejection forms down with him to the steamers.

He looked up Peter's name in the *Red Book*, *Who's Who*, *Burke*, the *Court Guide*, and what not, and finding it absent from all these, he took it for granted that there was no necessity for any special courtesies; Peter therefore, fifteen days after sending off his poem, received an envelope whose stamp illustrated the conquest of the Philippines by an Armed Liberty, while in the top left-hand corner were printed these simple words: "If not delivered within three days, please return to Box 257, Boston, Mass., U.S.A."

He was very pleased to get this letter. It was the first reply he had ever got from an editor, and he took it up unopened to the Holborn, to read it during lunch. But there was very little to read. The original verse had folded round it a nice half-sheet of cream-laid notepaper, with a gold *fleur de lis* in the corner, and underneath the motto, "Devoir Fera"; then, in the middle of the sheet, three or four lines of fine copperplate engraving, printed also in gold, and running as follows:—

"The editor of *Culture* regrets that he is unable to accept the enclosed contribution; it must not be imagined that any adverse criticism or suggestion is thereby passed upon the work; pressure of space, the previous acceptation of similar matter, and other causes having necessarily to be considered."

Peter was so much encouraged by this, that he sent his verses at once to Mr. McGregor, changing, however, the word "rude" in the fourth line to "rough," and adding a comma after "rapt," points insignificant in themselves perhaps, but indicative of a critic's ear, and certain (as he thought) to catch the approval of the distinguished scholar. In twenty-four hours he got his reply in the shape of an affectionate letter, enclosing his MSS.:—

"My dear Peter,

"No; I should be doing an injustice to my readers if I were to print your verse in the *Doctrinaire;* but you must not be discouraged by this action on my part. You are still very young, and no one who has followed (as you may be sure I have) your brilliant career at the University can doubt your ultimate success in whatever profession you undertake. But the path of letters is a stony one, and the level of general utility in such work is only reached by the most arduous efforts. I saw your Aunt Phœbe the other day, and she was warm in your praises. She told me you were thinking of becoming an architect; I sincerely hope you will, for I believe you have every aptitude for that profession. Plod on steadily and I wlll go warrant for your writing verse with the best of them. It is *inevitable,* my dear Peter, that one's early verse should be imitative and weak; but you have the 'inner voice,' do but follow the gleam and never allow your first enthusiasms to grow dim.

"Always your Father's Old Friend,

"ARCHIBALD WELLINGTON McGREGOR."

Peter was a little pained by this; but he answered it very politely, inviting himself to lunch on the following Thursday, and then, turning to his verses, he gave the title "Dead," and sent them to the *Patriot*, from whom he got no reply for a month.

He then wrote to the editor of the *Patriot* on a postcard, and said that, in view of the present deplorable reaction in politics, he feared the verses, if they were held over much longer, would lose their point. Would the *Patriot* be so kind, then, as to let him know what they proposed to do with the Poem?

He got a reply the same evening:—

"Telephone 239. "36A, Clare Market,
"Telegraph, 'Vindex.' "W.C.

"Dr. Sir,

"Your estd. favor to hand. No stamp being enclosed with verses, we have retained same, but will forward on receipt of two stamps, including cost of this.

"Faithfully yrs.,
"ALPHONSE RIPHRAIM.

"Please note change of address."

By this Peter Gurney was so angered, that he walked straight over to his club, rang up No. 239, and told the editor of the *Patriot*, personally, by word of mouth, and with emphasis, that he was a Pro-Boer; then he rang off before that astonished foreigner had time to reply.

But men of Mr. Peter Gurney's stamp are not cast down by these reverses. He remembered one rather low and insignificant sheet called the *Empire*, in which a vast number of unknown names had been appearing at the bottom of ballads, sonnets, and so forth, dealing mainly with the foreign policy of Great

Britain, to which country (as being their native land) the writers were apparently warmly attached.

Peter Gurney flattered himself that he understood why the *Empire* made a speciality of beginners. It was a new paper with little capital, and thought (wisely enough) that if it printed many such juvenilia it would, among the lot, strike some vein of good verse. He had heard of such ventures in journalism, and remembered being told that certain sonnets of Mr. Lewis Morris, and even the earlier poems of Tennyson, were thus buried away in old magazines. He copied out his verses once more, gave them the new title "Aspiro," and sent them to the *Empire*. He got a very polite letter in reply:—

> "Dear Mr. —— I have read your verses with much pleasure, and see by them that the praise I have heard on all sides of your unpublished work was not unmerited. Unfortunately, the *Empire* cannot afford to pay anything for its verse; and so large has been the demand upon our space, that we have been compelled to make it a rule that all contributions of this nature should pay a slight premium to obtain a space in our columns. But for this it would be impossible to distinguish between competitors without the risk of heartburnings and petty jealousies. We enclose our scale of charges, which are (as you see) purely nominal, and remain, awaiting your order to print,
>
> "Yours truly,
>
> "WILLIAM POWER."

I need hardly tell you that Peter, on receiving this letter, put two farthings into an envelope addressed to William Power, and was careful not to register or stamp it.

As for his Poem, he changed the title to "They

Live!" and sent it to the editor of *Criticism.* Next day he was not a little astonished to get his verses back, folded up in the following waggish letter:—

"The Laurels,
"20, Poplar Grove,
"S.W.
"Monday, the 21st of April.
"Sir,

"I am directed by the editor
To say that lack of space and press of matter
Forbid his using your delightful verses,
Which, therefore, he returns. Believe me still
Very sincerely yours, Nathaniel Pickersgill."

Now not a little disconsolate, young Mr. Gurney went out into the street, and thought of *Shavings* as a last chance. *Shavings* gave a guinea to the best poem on a given subject, and printed some of the others sent in. This week he remembered the subject was a eulogy of General Whitelock. He did not hesitate, therefore, to recast his poem, and to call it a "Threnody" on that commander, neglecting, by a poetic fiction, the fact that he was alive, and even looking well after his eight months of hard work against the Warra-Muggas. He went into the great buildings where *Shavings* is edited, and saw a young man opening with immense rapidity a hand-barrowful of letters, while a second sorted them with the speed of lightning, and a third tied them into neat bundles of five hundred each, and placed them in pigeon-holes under their respective initial letters.

"Pray, sir," said Peter to the first of these three men, "what are you doing?" "I am," replied the functionary, "just finishing my week's work" (for it was a Saturday morning), "and in the course of these four hours alone I am proud to say that I have opened no less than seven thousand three hundred and two poems on our great Leader, some of which, indeed, have been drawn from the principal English poets, but the greater part of which are, I am glad to say, original."

Embittered by such an experience, my friend Gurney returned to his home, and wrote that same afternoon the Satire on Modern Literature, in which he introduces his own verses as an example and warning, and on which, as all the world knows, his present fame reposes.

To-day everyone who reads these lines is envious of Mr. Peter Gurney's fame. He is the leader of the whole Cobbley school, the master of his own cousin, Mr. Peter Davey, and without question the model upon which Mr. Henry Hawk, Mr. Daniel Witton, and Mr. John Stuart have framed their poetic manner. He suffered and was strong. He condescended to prose, and kept his verse in reserve. The result no poet can ignore.

I should but mislead the student were I to pretend that Mr. Peter Gurney achieved his present reputation—a reputation perhaps somewhat exaggerated, but based upon real merit and industry—by any spontaneous effort. Hard, regular, unflinching labour in this, as in every other profession, is the condition of success. But the beginner may say (and with justice), "It is not enough to tell me to work; how should I set about it? What rules should I follow?" Let me pursue my invariable custom, and set down in the simplest and most methodical form the elements of the Short Lyric.

The student will, at some time or another, have suffered strong emotions. He will have desired to give them metrical form. He will have done so—and commonly he will have gone no further. I have before as I write a verse, the opening of one of the most unsuccessful poems ever written. It runs:—

"I am not as my fathers were,
I cannot pass from sleep to sleep,
Or live content to drink the deep
Contentment of the common air."

This is very bad. It is bad because it proceeded from a deep emotion only, and shot out untrammelled. It has no connection with verse as an art, and yet that art lies open for any young man who will be patient and humble, and who will *learn*.

His first business is to decide at once between the only two styles possible in manufactured verse, the Obscure and the Prattling. I say "the *only* two styles" because I don't think you can tackle the Grandiose, and I am quite certain you couldn't manage the Satiric. I know a young man in Red Lion Square who can do the Grandiose very well, and I am going to boom him when I think the time has come; but the Student-in-Ordinary cannot do it, so he may put it out of his head.

I will take the Simple or Prattling style first. Choose a subject from out of doors, first because it is the fashion, and secondly because you can go and observe it closely. For you must know that manufactured verse is very like drawing, and in both arts you have to take a model and be careful of details. Let us take (*e.g.*) a Pimpernel.

A Pimpernel is quite easy to write about; it has remarkable habits, it is not gross or common. It would be much harder to write about grass, for instance, or parsley.

First you write down anything that occurs to you, like this:—

> "Pretty little Pimpernel,
> May I learn to love you well?"

You continue on the style of "Twinkle, twinkle."

> "Hiding in the mossy shade,
> Like a lamp of — ᴗ made,
> Or a gem by fairies dropt
> In their . . "

and there you stick, just as you had got into the style of the "L'Allegro." I have no space or leisure to give the student the full treatment of so great a subject, how he would drag in the closing and opening of the flower, and how (skilfully avoiding the word "dell") he would end his ten or fifteen lines by a repetition of the first (an essential feature of the Prattling style). I will confine myself to showing him what may be made of these ridiculous six lines.

The first has an obvious fault. It runs too quickly, and one falls all over it. We will keep "Little" and put it first, so one might write "Little Purple Pimpernel." But even that won't do, though the alliteration is well enough. What change can we make?

It is at this point that I must introduce you to a most perfect principle. It is called the Mutation of Adjectives—it is almost the whole art of Occ. verse.

This principle consists in pulling out one's first obvious adjective, and replacing it by another of similar length, *chosen because it is peculiar.* You must not put in an adjective that could not possibly apply; for instance, you must not speak of the "Ponderous Rabbit" or the "Murky Beasts;" your adjective must be applicable, but it must be startling, as "The Tolerant Cow," "The Stammering Minister," or "The Greasy Hill"—all quite true and most unexpected.

Now, here it is evident that Purple is commonplace. What else can we find about the Pimpernel that is quite true and yet really startling? Let us (for instance) call it "tasteless." There you have it, "Little tasteless Pimpernel"—no one could read that too quickly, and it shows at the same time great knowledge of nature.

I will not weary you with every detail of the process, but I will write down *my* result after all the rules have been properly attended to. Read this, and see whether the lines do not fit with my canons of art, especially in what is called the "choice of words:"—

> "Little tasteless Pimpernel,
> Shepherd's Holt and warning spell
> Crouching in the cushat shade
> Like a mond of mowry made. . . ."

and so forth. There you have a perfect little gem. Nearly all the words are curious and well chosen, and yet the metre trips along like a railway carriage. The simplicity lies in the method; the quaint diction is quarried from Mr. Skeats' excellent book on etymology; but I need not point out any particular work, as your "Thesaurus" in this matter is for your own choosing.

So much for the Prattling style.

As for the Obscure style, it is so easy that it is getting overdone, and I would not depend too much upon it.

In its origins, it was due to the vagaries of some gentlemen and ladies who suffered from an imperfect education, and wrote as they felt, without stopping to think.

But that first holy rapture cannot be recovered. We must work by rule. The rules attaching to this kind of work are six:—

(1) Put the verb in the wrong place (some leave it out altogether);

(2) Use words that may be either verbs or nouns—plurals are very useful;

(3) Punctuate insufficiently;

(4) Make a special use of phrases that have two or three meanings;

(5) Leave out relatives;

(6) Have whole sentences in apposition.

Some of our young poets have imagined that the mere use of strange words made up the Obscure style. I need not say that they were wrong. Thus, the lines—

> "And shall I never tread them more,
> My murrant balks of wealden lathes?"

are singularly bad. Anyone could be obscure in so simple a fashion. It behoves the student rather to read carefully such lines as the following, in which I have again tackled the Pimpernel, this time in the Obscure manner.

I begin with "What Pimpernels," which might mean "What! Pimpernels?" or, "*What* Pimpernels?" or again, "What *Pimpernels!*"; expressing surprise, or a question, or astonished admiration: but do you think I am going to give the show away by telling the reader what I mean? Not a bit of it. There is something in our island temper which loves mystery: something of the North. I flatter myself I can do it thoroughly:—

> "What Pimpernels; a rare indulgence blesses
> The winter wasting in imperfect suns
> And Pimpernels are in the waning, runs
> A hand unknown the careless winter dresses,
> Not for your largess to the ruined fells,
> Her floors in waste, I call you, Pimpernels."

There! I think that will do very fairly well. One can make sense out of it, and it is broad and full, like a modern religion; it has many aspects, and it makes men think. There is not one unusual word, and the second line is a clear and perfect bit of English. Yet how deep and solemn and thorough is the whole!

And yet, for all my ability in these matters, I may not offer an example for the reader to follow. I am conscious of something more powerful (within this strict channel), and I am haunted reproachfully by a great soul. May I quote what none but She could have written? It is the most perfect thing that modern England knows. Every lesson I might painfully convey there stands manifest, of itself, part of the Created Thing.

THE YELLOW MUSTARD.

OH! ye that prink it to and fro,
In pointed flounce and furbelow,
What have ye known, what can ye know
That have not seen the mustard grow?

The yellow mustard is no less
Than God's good gift to loneliness;
And he was sent in gorgeous press,
To jangle keys at my distress.

I heard the throstle call again
Come hither, Pain! come hither, Pain!
Till all my shameless feet were fain
To wander through the summer rain.

And far apart from human place,
And flaming like a vast disgrace,
There struck me blinding in the face
The livery of the mustard race.

. . . . .

To see the yellow mustard grow
Beyond the town, above, below;
Beyond the purple houses, oh!
To see the yellow mustard grow!

THE INTERVIEW.

It is now some years ago since I was sitting in Mr. Caliban's study, writing in his name upon the Balance of Power in Europe. I had just completed my article, and passed it to him to sign, when I noticed that he was too much absorbed in a book which he was reading to pay attention to my gesture.

Men of his stamp enforce courtesy in others by their mere presence. It would have been impossible to have disturbed him. I turned to a somewhat more lengthy composition, which was also to appear above his signature, entitled, "The Effect of Greek Philosophy upon European Thought." When I had completed my analysis of this profound historical influence, I thought that my master and guide would have freed himself from the net of the author who thus entranced him. I was mistaken. I had, however, but just begun a third article, of which the subject escapes me, when he turned to me and said, closing the book between his hands:

"Will you go and interview someone for me?"

I fear my sudden change of expression betrayed the fact that the idea was repugnant to one familiar rather with foreign politics and with the Classics than with the reporters' side of the paper.

Mr. Caliban looked at my collar with his kindly eyes, and kept them fixed upon it for some seconds. He then smiled (if such a man could be said to smile) and continued:

"I want to tell you something . . ."

There was profound silence for a little while, during which a number of thoughts passed through my mind. I remembered that Dr. Caliban was Editor at that moment of the *Sunday Herald*. I remembered that I was his right hand, and that without me the enormous labour he weekly undertook could never have been accomplished without trespassing upon the sanctity of the Sabbath. After a little hesitation, he pulled down his waistcoat, hitched his trousers at the knees, crossed his legs, made a half-turn towards me (for his study-chair was mounted upon a swivel), and said:

"It's like this:— . . ."

I assured him that I would do what he wished, for I knew, whenever he spoke in this tone, that there was something to be done for England.

"It's like this," he went on, "I have found a man here who should *count*, who should *tell*. It is a fearful thought that such a mind can have remained so long hidden. Here is a man with something in him quite peculiar and apart—and he is unknown! It is England through and through, and the best of England; it is more than that. Even where I disagree with him, I find something like a living voice. He gets right at one, as it were . . . yet I never heard his name!"

Here Mr. Caliban, having stopped for a moment, as though seeking something in his memory, declaimed in a rich monotone:

> "Full many a gem of purest ray serene
> The dark unfathomed caves of ocean bear:
> Full many a flower is born to blush unseen
> And waste its sweetness on the desert air."

There was a little silence. Then he said abruptly:

"Do you know Wordsworth's definition of a poet? Take it down. I should like you to use it."

I pulled out my note-book and wrote in shorthand from his dictation a sublime phrase, which was new to me: "*A Poet is a* MAN *speaking to* MEN."

"This man," said Dr. Caliban simply, "is a man speaking to men."

He put the book into my hands; two or three of the leaves were turned down, and on each page so marked was a passage scored in pencil. The lines would have arrested my eye even, had a greater mind than my own not selected them.

"*A woman is only a woman, but a good cigar is a smoke.*"

"*Tied wrist to bar for their red iniquitee.*"

"*To do butcher work*" (he is speaking of war) "*yer don't want genlemen, 'cept to lead.*"

"*I got the gun-barrels red-hot and fetched the whipcord out of the cupboard, while the other man held the screaming, writhing thing down upon the floor.*"

"*Under whose* (speaking of God) *awful hand we hold dominion over palm and pine.*"

I have no space to quote a longer passage of verse, evidently intended to be sung to a banjo, and describing the emotions of the author in a fit of delirium tremens when he suffered from the hallucination that a red-hot brass monkey was himself attempting song. The poet showed no jealousy of the animal. There was the full, hearty Anglo-Saxon friendship for a comrade and even for a rival, and I met the same tone again on a further page in the line:

"You're a better man than I am, Gunga Din."

I looked up at Mr. Caliban and said:

"Well?":—for these short phrases are often the most emphatic.

"Well," said Dr. Caliban, "that man must not be allowed to go under. He must be made, and we must make him."

I said that such a man could not fail to pierce through and conquer. He seemed the very salt and marrow of all that has made us great.

Dr. Caliban laid his hand in a fatherly way upon my shoulder and said:

"You are still young; you do not know how long fame may take to find a man, if the way is not pointed out to her; and if she takes too long, sometimes he dies of a broken heart."

It was a noble thought in one who had known Fame almost from the very day when, as a lad of 22 years old, he had stood up in the chapel at Barking Level and answered the preacher with the words, "Lord, here am I."

Dr. Caliban continued in a few simple words to convince me that my foolish pride alone stood between this young genius and the fame he deserved. He pointed out what a weight would lie upon my mind were that poet some day to become famous, and to be able to say when I presented myself at his receptions:

"Get ye hence: I know ye not!"

He added the awful words that death might find us at any moment, and that then we should have to answer, not for our reasons or our motives, but for the things we have done, and for the things we have left undone. He added that he would regard a visit to this new writer as overtime work, and that he was ready to pay my expenses, including cab fares to and from the station. He ended with an appeal which would have convinced one less ready to yield: a magnificent picture of the Empire and of the Voice for which it had waited so long.

. . . .

It seems unworthy, after the relation of this intimate domestic scene, to add any words of exhortation to the reader and student.

I will not pretend that the interview is a form of true literature. If I have been guilty of too great a confidence, my excess has proceeded from an earnest desire to watch over others of my kind, and to warn them lest by one chance refusal they should destroy the opportunities of a lifetime.

To interview another, even a rival, is sometimes necessary at the outset of a career. It is an experience that need not be repeated. It is one that no earnest student of human nature will regret.

The powerful emotions aroused by the reminiscence of Dr. Caliban's eloquence, and of the meeting to which it led, must not be desecrated by too lengthy an insistance upon the mere technique of a subsidiary branch of modern letters. I will state very briefly my conclusions as to what is indispensable in the regulation of this kind of literature.

It is, in the first place, of some moment that the young interviewer should take his hat and gloves with him in his left hand into the room. If he carries an umbrella or cane, this also should be carried in the same hand, leaving the right hand completely free. Its readiness for every purpose is the mark of a gentleman, and the maintenance of that rank is absolutely necessary to the *sans gêne* which should accompany a true interview.

In the second place, let him, the moment he appears, explain briefly the object of his visit. Without any such introduction as "The fact is . . ." "It is very odd, but . . .", let him say plainly and simply, like an Englishman, "I have been sent to interview you on the part of such and such a paper."

He will then be handed (in the majority of cases) a short type-written statement, which he will take into his right hand, pass into his left, in among the gloves, stick, hat, &c., and will bow, not from the shoulders, nor from the hips, but subtly from the central vertebrae.

In the third place he will go out of the room.

There are two exceptions to this general procedure. The first is with men quite unknown; the second with men of high birth or great wealth.

In the first case, the hat and gloves should be laid upon a table and the stick leaning against it in such a way as not to fall down awkwardly in the middle of a conversation. The student will then begin to talk in a genial manner loudly, and will continue for about half-an-hour; he will end by looking at his watch, and will go away and write down what he feels inclined.

In the second case, he will do exactly the same, but with a different result, for in the first case he will very probably become the friend of the person interviewed, which would have happened anyhow, and in the second case he will be forbidden the house, a result equally inevitable.

I cannot conclude these remarks without exhorting the young writer most earnestly, when he is entering upon the first of these distressing experiences, to place a firm trust in Divine Providence, and to remember that, come what may, he has done his duty.

If he should have any further hesitation as to the general manner in which an interview should be written, he has but to read what follows. It constitutes the interview which I held with that young genius whom Mr. Caliban persuaded me to visit, and of whose fame I shall therefore always feel myself a part.

INTERVIEW

WITH HIM.

(Written specially for the *Sunday Englishman*, by the Rev. JAMES CALIBAN, D.D.) *

"*By the peace among the peoples, men shall know ye serve the Lord.*"—DEUTERONOMY xvi. 7.

. . . Leaping into a well-appointed cab, I was soon whirled to a terminus which shall be nameless, not a hundred miles from Brandon Street, and had the good luck to swing myself into the guard's van just as the train was steaming out from the platform. I plunged at once *in medias res*, and some two hours later alit in the sunny and growing residential town of Worthing. I hailed a vehicle which plied for hire, and begged the driver to conduct me to 29, Darbhai Road, "if indeed," to quote my own words to the Jehu, "if indeed it be worth a drive. I understand it is close upon a mile."

"Yes, sir," replied the honest fellow, "You will find, sir, that it is quite a mile, sir. Indeed, sir, we call it a little over a mile, sir."

I was soon whirled, as fast as the type of carriage permitted, to Laburnum Lodge, Darbhai Road, where a neat-handed Phyllis smilingly opened the door for me, and took my card up to her master, bidding me be seated awhile in the hall. I had the leisure to notice that it was lit by two stained glass

* I reproduce the title in its original form. I was only too pleased to know that my work would appear above his signature; nor do I see anything reprehensible in what is now a recognized custom among journalists.

panels above the entrance, representing Alfred the Great and Queen Victoria. In a few minutes the servant returned with the message that her master would be down in a moment, and begged me to enter his parlour until he could attend me, as he was just then in his study, looking out of window at a cricket match in an adjoining field.

I found myself in a richly-furnished room, surrounded by curious relics of travel, and I was delighted to notice the little characteristic touches that marked the personal tastes of my host. Several skulls adorned the walls, and I observed that any natural emotion they might cause was heightened by a few tasteful lines such as actors paint upon their faces. Thus one appeared to grin beyond the ordinary, another was fitted with false eyes, and all had that peculiar subtle expression upon which genius loves to repose in its moments of leisure. I had barely time to mark a few more notable matters in my surroundings, when I was aware that I was in the presence of my host.

"No," or "Yes," said the great man, smiling through his spectacles and puffing a cloud of smoke towards me in a genial fashion, "I do not in the least mind telling you how it is done. I do not think," he added drily, "that any other fellows will pull quite the same chock-a-block haul, even if I do give them the fall of the halyard. You must excuse these technical terms; I make it a point to speak as I write—I think it is more natural."

I said I should be delighted to excuse him,

"I hope you will also excuse," he continued, "my throwing myself into my favourite attitude."

I said that, on the contrary, I had long wished to see it.

With a sigh of relief he thrust those creative hands of his into his trouser pockets, slightly stooped his shoulders, and appeared to my delight exactly as he does in the photograph he handed me for publication.

"To show you how it is done, I cannot begin better than by a little example," he said.

He went to a neighbouring table, rummaged about in a pile of the *Outlook* and *Vanity Fair*, and produced a scrap of paper upon which there was a type-written poem. His hands trembled with pleasure, but he controlled himself well (for he is a strong, silent kind of man), and continued:—

"I will not weary you with the whole of this Work. I am sure you must already be familiar with it. In the Volunteer camp where I was recently staying, and where I slept under canvas like anybody else, the officers knew it by heart, and used to sing it to a tune of my own composition (for you must know that I write these little things to airs of my own). I will only read you the last verse, which, as is usual in my lyrics, contains the pith of the whole matter."

Then in a deep voice he intoned the following, with a slightly nasal accent which lent it a peculiarly individual flavour:—

"I'm sorry for Mister Naboth;
I'm sorry to make him squeak;
But the Lawd above me made me strawng
In order to pummel the weak."

"That chorus, which applies to one of the most important problems of the Empire, contains nearly all the points that illustrate 'How it is Done.' In the first place, note the conception of the Law. It has been my effort to imprint this idea of the Law upon the mind of the English-speaking world—a phrase, by the way, far preferable to that of Anglo-Saxon, which I take this opportunity of publicly repudiating. You may, perhaps, have noticed that my idea of the Law is the strongest thing in modern England. 'Do this because I tell you, or it will be the worse for you,' is all we know, and all we need to know. For so, it seems to me, Heaven" (here he reverently raised the plain billy-cock hat which he is in the habit of wearing in his drawing-room) "governs the world, and we who are Heaven's lieutenants can only follow upon the same lines. I will not insist upon the extent to which the religious training I enjoyed in early youth helped to cast me in that great mould. You have probably noticed its effect in all my work."

I said I had.

"Well, then, first and foremost, I have in this typical instance brought out my philosophy of the Law. In my private conversation I call this 'following the gleam.'"

"Now for the adventitious methods by which I enhance the value of my work. Consider the lilt. 'Lilt' is the 'Túm ti ti túm ti túm' effect which you may have felt in my best verse."

I assured him I had indeed felt it.

"Lilt," he continued, "is the hardest thing of all to acquire. Thousands attempt it, and hundreds fail. I have it (though I say it who should not) to perfection. It is the quality you will discover in the old ballads, but there it is often marred by curious accidents which I can never properly explain. Their metre is often very irregular, and I fancy that their style (which my Work closely resembles) has suffered by continual copying. No: where you get the true 'Lilt' is in the music halls—I am sorry it is so often wasted upon impertinent themes. Do you know 'It is all very fine and large,' or 'At my time of life,' or again, 'Now we shan't be long'?"

I answered I had them all three by heart.

"I shouldn't say they were worth *that*," he answered, as a shade of disappointment appeared upon his delicate, mobile features, "but there is a place where you get it to perfection, and that is Macaulay's *Lays of Ancient Rome*. They are my favourite reading. But that is another story."

"To turn to quite a different point, the Vernacular. It isn't everything that will go down in ordinary English. Of course I *do* use ordinary English—at least, Bible English, in my best work. For instance, there is a little thing called "In the Confessional," which I propose to read to you later, and which has no slang nor swear-words from beginning to end."

"But, of course, that is quite an exception. Most things won't stand anything but dialect, and I just give you this tip gratis. You can make anything individual and strong by odd spelling. It arrests the attention, and you haven't got to pick your words. Did you ever read a beautiful work called *Colorado Bill; or, From Cowboy to President?* Well, I can assure you that when it was in English, before being turned into dialect, it was quite ordinary-like."

"But that ain't all. One has now and then to strike a deeper note, and striking a deeper note is so simple, that I wonder it has not occurred to others of our poets. You have got to imagine yourself in a church, and you must read over your manuscript to yourself in that kind of hollow voice—you know what I mean."

I swore that I did.

"*Now*, you see why one puts 'ye' for 'you,' and 'ye be' for 'you are,' and mentions the Law in so many words. It is not very difficult to do, and when one does succeed, one gets what I call A1 copper-bottomed poetry."

He went to a corner of the room, opened a large, scented, velvet-bound book upon a brass reading-desk, looked at me severely, coughed twice, and began as follows:

"I am about to read you 'In the Confessional.' The greatest critic of the century has called this the greatest poem of the century. I begin at the third verse, and the seventeenth line:—

. . . . .

"Lest he forget the great ally
In heaven yclept hypocrisy,
So help me Bawb! I'll mark him yet—
Lest he forget! Lest he forget!"

. . . . .

He closed the book with becoming reverence.

And there was a silence, during which the grand words went on running in my head as their author had meant them to do. "Lest he forget! Lest he forget!" Ah, may heaven preserve its darling poet, and never let him fall from the height of that great message.

"Well," said he, genially, anticipating my applause, "Good-bye. But before you go please let me beg you to tell the public that I lately wrote something for the *Times* a great deal better than anything else I have ever written. Nobody seems to read the *Times*," he continued, in a tone of slight petulance, "and I have not seen it quoted anywhere. I wonder if it is properly known? Please tell people that that little note about 'copyright' is only for fun. *Anyone* may use it who likes—I had a paragraph put in the papers to say so. It's like this—" He then added a few conventional words of God-speed, and I left him. I have never seen him since.

And yet . . . and yet . . .

The student will now pardon me, I trust, if I go somewhat more deeply into things than is customary in text books of this class. That little conquest over pride, that little task honestly performed, earned me something I shall value for ever, something that will be handed down in our family "even unto the third and the fourth generation" (*Habb.* vii. 13). It is something that means far, far more to me than a mere acquaintance with an author could possibly have done. For who can gauge so volatile a thing as friendship? Who could with certitude have pointed me out and said, "There goes *His* friend"? The Written Thing remained.

In my room, nay, just above me as I write, hangs framed the following note in pencil.

"Awfully glad to see the stuff in the 'Herald,' but say—are you old Caliban? That was rather stiff on a jack high? Wasn't it? Never mind. You didn't ask me for my auto, but I send it herewith right along, for I *like* you."

There is the Man Alone as He IS—. . . It seems of small moment, but there is something more. Framed in dark oak and gold very sumptuously, and hanging quite apart, is the little shred of paper which He enclosed. Shall I whisper what is written upon it? . . .? . . . The first few jotted notes of the glorious song which rang through the Empire like a bugle-call, and hurled it at Nicaragua.

Hark and attend my Chosen: Ye have heard me — *Mem.—Can a preposition begin with a capital?*
ye *people*
Out of the East,
with an introduction?
I came and the nations trembled: I bore the Mark — *Mem.—Alternative, "with a bag and a blanket."*
with a [illegible]
[illegible]
glory about me?
of the Beast,

And I made ye a hundred books—yea! even an hundred and one — *Good!*
Of all the labours of men that labour under the sun.

Second "yea"? Uncle says "delete."

And I clad me about with Terrors: Yea! I
covered my paths with dread,
And the women-folk were astonied at the horrible
things I said:

And the men of the Island Race were some of
them woundily bored,
But the greater part of them paid me well: and
I praised the Lord.
And when—as the spirit was full—I sniggered
and lapped and swore
As ever did men before me, men of the days of
yore.
(?)
When-as the spirit was full—But when it was
rare and low
I copied the Psalms at random; and lo! it was
even so!

Dick says "Days of Yore" is commonplace. Tore? Gore? Lore? More? provisional: see Emily also about it.

(*Fill in here: ask* [illegible])
Publisher

Then up and arose the Daughter-Nations: Up and
arose
Fearless men reciting me fearlessly through the
nose,
Some of them Presbyterian, and some of them
Jews, and some
Of the Latter-Day Church, King Solomon's sect
—which is awfully rum.
(*Stuck.*)

Uncle says that repetition is Greek. Mem.—plagiarism?

Frivolous. Change.

. . . the lot of it . . . Anglo-Saxons . . . shout it
aloud
. . . at it again? . . . back the crowd?
(*Fill in. Mem.—must be consecutive*)

Things are not as they were (*common-place*)
. . . . (*delete*)
Things are not as they . . . Things and the
Change . . .
Things and . . . things . . .
(*Leave this to fill in*)

* * * * * *

And some of ye stand at a wicket, and they are
the luckier men,
But others field afar on a field, and ever and then,
When-as the over is over, they cross to the other
side,

Whenas. Good. Mem.—use in "Horeb."

A weary thing to the flesh and a wounding thing
to the pride.
And Cabinet Ministers play at a game ye should
all avoid,

He will have to g'.

It is played with youngling bats and a pellet of
celluloid,
And a little net on a table, and is known as the
named (*better*)
PING and the PONG.
England, Daughter of Sion, why do you do this
wrong?
And some, like witherless Frenchmen, circle
around in rings,
England, Daughter of Sion, why do you do these
things?
Why do you . . .
(*Mem.—after Uncle to-morrow. Billy's: refuse
terms.*)

These are the chance lines as they came—the disjointed words—everything—just as He wrote them down.

Reader—or whatever you be—was that a small reward? Are you willing *now* to say that Interviewing has no wages of its own? Will you sneer at it as unfit to take its place in your art? Truly, "Better is he that humbleth himself than a pillar of brass, and a meek heart than many fastenings."

THE PERSONAL PAR.

CLOSELY connected with the Interview, and forming a natural sequel to any treatise upon that Exercise, is the Personal Par. It contains, as it were, all the qualities of the Interview condensed into the smallest possible space; it advertises the subject, instructs the reader, and is a yet sharper trial of the young writer's character.

The homely advice given in the preceding section, where mention was made of "pride" and of "pockets," applies with far more force to the Personal Par. With the Interview, it is well to mask one's name; with the Personal Par, it is absolutely necessary to conceal it. The danger the author runs is an attraction to Mrs. Railston, who in her book strongly advises this form of sport—she herself does Bess in *All About Them*. On the other hand, Lieut.-Col. Lory says, in his *Journalist's Vade-mecum* (p. 63): "A Personal Par should never be penned by the Aspirant to Literary honours. Undetected, it renders life a burden of suspense; detected, it spells ruin."* He quotes twenty-five well-known peers and financiers who rose by steadily refusing to do this kind of work during their period of probation on the press.

* Let the student note, by way of warning, and avoid this officer's use of ready-made phrases.

The present guide, which is final, will run to no such extremes. Secrecy is indeed essential; yet there are three excellent reasons for writing Personal Pars, at least in early youth.

(1.) The Personal Par is the easiest to produce of all forms of literature. Any man or woman, famous or infamous for any reason, is a subject ready to hand, and to these may be added all persons whatsoever living, dead, or imaginary; and anything whatever may be said about them. Editors, in their honest dislike of giving pain, encourage the inane, and hence more facile, form of praise. Moreover, it takes but a moment to write, and demands no recourse to books of reference.

(2.) The Personal Par can always be placed—if not in England, then in America. Though written in any odd moments of one's leisure time, it will always represent money; and the whole of the period from July to October, when ordinary work is very slack, can be kept going from the stock one has by one.

(3.) It has a high economic value, not only in the price paid for it, but indirectly, as an advertisement. This is a point which Lieut.-Col. Lory and Mrs. Railston both overlook.

A short specimen, written in August, 1885, at the very beginning of the movement, by my friend, Mrs. Cowley (the Folk-Lorist, not the Poetess), for the *Gazette*, will make these three points clear:—

"The capture of that rare bird, the Cross-tailed Eagle, which is cabled from St. Fandango's, recalls the fact that the famous Picture "Tiny Tots" was formerly in the possession of the present Governor of that island. The picture is put up to auction by Messrs. Philpots next Saturday, and, judging by the public attendance at their galleries during the last fortnight, the bidding should be brisk."

There is no such bird as the Cross-tailed Eagle, nor any such person as the Governor of St. Fandango's, nor indeed is there even any such island. Yet Mrs. Cowley was paid 5*s*. by the *Gazette* for her little bit of research; it was copied into most of the papers, with acknowledgment, and she got a commission from Messrs. Philpots. The former owner of "Tiny Tots" (Mr. Gale of Kew, a wealthy man) wrote a long and interesting letter explaining that some error had been made, and that not he, but his wife's father, had been an *Inspector** (not Governor) in *St. Vincent's*. He begged the writer to call on him—her call was the origin of a life-long friendship, and Mrs. Cowley was mentioned in his will.

I must detain the student no longer with what is, after all, a very small corner of our art, but conclude with a few carefully chosen examples before proceeding to the next section on Topographical Essays.

Examples.

Wit and Wisdom of the Upper Classes.

Her Royal Highness the Hereditary Grand Duchess of Solothurn was driving one day down Pall Mall when she observed a poor pickpocket plying his precarious trade. Stopping the carriage immediately,

* Of what?

she asked him gently what she could do for him. He was dumbfounded for a reply, and, withdrawing his hand from the coat-tail of an elderly major, managed to mumble out that he was a widower with a wife and six children who were out of work and refused to support him, though earning excellent wages. This reasoning so touched the Princess, that she immediately gave him a place as boot-black in the Royal Palace of Kensington. Discharged from this position for having prosecuted H.R.H. for six months' arrears of wages, he set up as a publican at the "Sieve and Pannier" at Wimbledon, a licence of some ten thousand pounds in value, and a standing example of the good fortune that attends thrift and industry.

* * *

It is not generally known that the late Lord Grumbletooth rose from the ranks. His lordship was a singularly reticent man, and the matter is still shrouded in obscurity. He was, however, a politician in the best sense of the word, and owed his advancement to the virtues that have made England famous. The collection of domestic china at Grumbletooth House will vie with any other collection at any similar house in the kingdom.

* * *

Dr. Kedge, whose death was recently announced in the papers, was the son of no less a personage than Mr. Kedge, of the Old Hall, Eybridge. It is hardly fair to call him a self-made man, for his father paid a considerable sum both for his education and for the settlement of his debts on leaving the University.

But he was a bright-eyed, pleasant host, and will long be regretted in the journalistic world.

* * *

Lady Gumm's kindness of heart is well known. She lately presented a beggar with a shilling, and then discovered that she had not the wherewithal to pay her fare home from Queen's Gate to 376, Park Lane (her ladyship's town house). Without a moment's hesitation she borrowed eighteen pence of the grateful mendicant, a circumstance that easily explains the persecution of which she has lately been the victim.

* * *

Lord Harmbury was lately discovered on the top of a 'bus by an acquaintance who taxed him with the misadventure. "I would rather be caught *on* a 'bus than *in* a trap," said the witty peer. The *mot* has had some success in London Society.

* * *

Mr. Mulhausen, the M.F.H. of the North Downshire Hunt, has recently written an article on "Falconry" for the *Angler's World*. The style of the "brochure" shows a great advance in "technique," and cannot fail to give a permanent value to his opinion on Athletics, Gentleman-farming, and all other manly sports and pastimes. Mr. Mulhausen is, by the way, a recently-elected member of the Rock-climbers' Club, and is devoted to Baccarat.

* * *

There is no truth in the rumour that Miss Finn-Coul, daughter of Colonel Wantage-Brown, was about to marry her father's second wife's son by an earlier marriage, Mr. James Grindle-Torby. The Colonel is a strong Churchman, and disapproves of such unions between close relatives; moreover, as C.O., he has forbidden the young lieutenant (for such is his rank) to leave the barracks for a fortnight, a very unusual proceeding in the Hussars.

* * *

Lady Sophia Van Huren is famous for her repartee. In passing through Grosvenor Gate an Irish beggar was heard to hope that she would die the black death of Machushla Shawn. A sharp reply passed her lips, and it is a thousand pities that no one exactly caught its tenor; it was certainly a gem.

* * *

It is well known that the Bishop of Pontygarry has no sympathy with the extreme party in the Church. Only the other day he was so incensed at a service held in Ribble-cum-Taut, that he fought the officiating clergyman for half an hour in his own garden, and extorted a complete apology. He also forbad anyone in the village ever to go to Church again, and himself attended the Methodist Chapel on the ensuing Sunday. Had we a few more prelates of the same mettle things would be in a very different condition.

THE TOPOGRAPHICAL ARTICLE.

THE Topographical Article is so familiar as to need but little introduction. . . . Personally, I do not recommend it; it involves a considerable labour; alone, of all forms of historical writing, it demands accuracy; alone, it is invariably un-paid.

Nevertheless, there are special occasions when it will be advisable to attempt it; as—in order to please an aged and wealthy relative; in order to strike up a chance acquaintance with a great Family; in order to advertise land that is for sale; in order to prevent the sale, or to lower the price (in these two last cases it is usual to demand a small fee from the parties interested); in order to vent a just anger; in order to repay a debt; in order to introduce a "special" advertisement for some manure or other; and so forth. Most men can recall some individual accident when a training in Topographical Writing would have been of value to them.

There even arise, though very rarely, conditions under which this kind of writing is positively ordered. Thus, when the Editor of the *Evening Mercury* changed his politics for money on the 17th of September, 1899, all that part of his staff who were unable to drop their outworn shibboleths were put on to writing up various parts of London in the legal interval preceding their dismissal, and a very good job they made of it.

Never, perhaps, were the five rules governing the art more thoroughly adhered to. A land-owning family was introduced into each; living persons were treated with courtesy and affection; a tone of regret was used at the opening of each; each closed with a phrase of passionate patriotism; and each was carefully run parallel to the course of English History in general; and the proper praise and blame allotted to this name and that, according to its present standing with the more ignorant of the general public.*

It was in this series (afterwards issued in Book form under the title, *London! My London*) that the following article—which I can put forward as an excellent model—was the contribution of my friend, Mr. James Bayley. It may interest the young reader (if he be as yet unfamiliar with our great London names) to know that under the pseudonym of "Cringle" is concealed the family of Holt, whose present head is, of course, the Duke of Sheffield.

DISAPPEARING LONDON: MANNING GREEN.

At a moment when a whole district of the metropolis is compulsorily passing into the hands of a soulless corporation, it is intolerable that the proprietors of land in that district should receive no compensation

* The student will find a list of Historical Personages to praise and blame carefully printed in two colours at the end of Williams' *Journalist's History of England*.

for the historical importance of their estates. Manning Green, which will soon be replaced by the roar and bustle—or bustle and confusion, whichever you like—of a great railway station, is one of those centres whence the great empire-builders of our race proceeded in past times.

For many centuries it was a bare, bleak spot, such as our England could boast by the thousand in the rude but heroic days when the marvellous fortunes of the Anglo-Saxon race were preparing in the slow designs of Providence. For perhaps a generation it was one of those suburban villages that are said by a contemporary poet to "nestle in their trees." Doubtless it sent forth in the sixties many brave lads to fight for the liberties of Europe in Italy or Denmark, but their humble record has perished. Such a thought recalls the fine lines of Gray:—

> "Some mute inglorious Milton here may rest;
> Some Cromwell guiltless of his country's blood."

Twenty to twenty-five years ago the advancing tide of the capital of the world swept round this little outlying place; it was submerged, and soon made part of greater London.

Relics are still to be discovered of the period when Manning Green had something rural about it, as Highgate and South Croydon have now. Thus "The Jolly Drover" (whose license was recently refused because it was not a tied house) recalls the great sheep-droves that once passed through the village from the north. It is now rare indeed to meet with a countryman driving his flock to market through the streets of London, though the sight is not absolutely unknown. The present writer was once stopped in the early morning by a herd of oxen south of Westminster Bridge, and what may seem more remarkable he has frequently seen wild animals in the charge of negroes pass through Soho on their way to the Hippodrome. It is as Tennyson says:—

> "The old order changes, giving place to the new,"

until at last

> "Beyond these voices there is peace."

Another relic of the old village of Manning Green is the Court Baron, which is still held (how few Londoners know this!) once a year, for the purpose of providing a small but regular income to a relative of the Lord Chancellor. This Court was probably not held before the year 1895, but it is none the less of extreme interest to antiquarians.

The first mention of Manning Green in history is in a letter to Edward Lord Cringle, the pioneer and ally of the beneficent reforms that remain inseparably associated with the name of the eighth Henry. This letter is written from prison by one Henry Turnbull, a yeoman, and contains these phrases:—

> "For that very certainly, my good Lord, I never did this thing, no, nor met the Friar nor had any dealing with him. And whatever I did that they say is treason I did it being a simple man, as following the Mass, which I know is welcome to the King's Majesty, and not knowing who it was that sang it, no, nor speaking to him after, as God knows. And, my dear Lord, I have had conveyed to you, as you know, my land of Horton with the Grey farm and *the mere called Foul Marsh or Manning*, having neither son nor any other

> but my own life only, and for that willingly would I give you this land, and so I have done; and, my good Lord, speak for me at Court in this matter, remembering my gift of the land. . . ."

This Turnbull was afterwards executed for treason at Tyburn. There is still a Turnbull in the parish, but as his father's name was Weissenstein he is very unlikely to have any connection with the original family of yeomen.

The land (if land it could then be called) did not, oddly enough, remain long in the Cringle family. It was sold by Lord Edward to the Carmelites, and on the dissolution of that order was returned by the grateful monarch to its original owner. We next find "Manning" or "Foul Marsh" drained during that period of active beneficence on the part of the great landlords which marked the seventeenth century. We are acquainted of this fact in our agricultural history by an action recorded in 1631, where it appears that one Nicholas Hedon had gone to shoot snipe, as had been once of common right in the manor, and had so trespassed upon land "now drained at his lordship's charges, and by him enclosed." Hedon lost both ears, and was pilloried.

Manning is probably alluded to also in a strong protest of the old Liberal blood* against ship-money, to which exaction it contributed 1*s.* 4*d.* The sum need not excite ridicule, as it represents quite 4*s.* of our present currency. The vigorous protest of the family against this extortion is one of the finest

* The Holts are still Liberal-Unionists.

examples of our sterling English spirit on the eve of the Civil War. The money was, however, paid.

In the troubles of the Civil Wars Manning (now no no longer a marsh, but a *green*) was sold to John Grayling, but the deed of conveyance being protested at the Restoration, it was restored to its original owners at the intruder's charge by an action of *Novel Disseizin*. After Monmouth's rebellion, Manning was in danger of suffering confiscation, and was hurriedly sold to a chance agent (William Greaves) at so low a price as to refute for ever all insinuations of rapacity upon the part of its now ducal owners. It was happily restored by a grateful nation as a free gift after the glorious Revolution of 1688, and the agent, who had only acquired it by taking advantage of the recent troubles, was very properly punished. King William congratulated the family in a famous epigram, which a natural ignorance of the Taal forbids us to transcribe.

In 1718, Manning being still pasture of a somewhat spongy nature (Guy, in his report, calls it "soggy and poor land, reedy, and fit for little"), there was a rumour that the New River canal would pass through it, and it was sold to Jonathan Hemp. The New River was proved, however, in the pleadings before both Houses of Parliament, to have no necessity for this canal, and Hemp was compelled (as it was a mere speculation on his part) to sell it back again to its distinguished owner at a merely nominal price.

Nothing further can be traced with regard to Manning Green (as it was now commonly called) till the report in 1780 that coal had been found beneath it. Such a deposit so near the metropolis naturally attracted the attention of merchants, and the Family sold the place for the last time to a merchant of the name of Hogg for £20,000.

The report proved false; yet, oddly enough, it was the beginning of Mr. Hogg's prosperity.

We have no space to dwell on this interesting character. "Hogg's Trustees" are an ecclesiastical household word in our principal watering-places, and the "Hogg Institute" at Brighton is a monument of Christian endeavour. He was a shrewd bargainer, a just man, and upon his mantel-pieces were to be discovered ornaments in alabaster representing Joshua and Richard Cœur de Lion.

The growth of the metropolis entered largely into Mr. Hogg's enlightened prevision of the future, and he obtained promises from a large number of people to build houses upon his land, which houses should, after a term of years, become his (Hogg's) property, and cease to belong to those who had paid to put them up. How Mr. Hogg managed to obtain such promises is still shrouded in mystery, but the universal prevalence of the system to-day in modern England would surely prove that there is something in our Imperial race which makes this form of charity an element of our power.

Mr. Hogg's only daughter married Sir John Moss, Lord Mayor; and Mr. Moss, the son, was the father of the present Lord Hemelthorpe. Thus something romantic still clings to poor Manning

Green, of which Lord Hemelthorpe was, until his recent bankruptcy, the proprietor.

There is little more to be said about Manning Green. The Ebenezer Chapel has a history of its own, written by the Rev. Napoleon Plaything, son of Mr. Honey Q. Plaything, of Bismark, Pa. The success of the boys' club has been detailed in *God's London*, by Mr. Zitali, of the "Mission to the Latin Races." The book is well worth buying, if only for this one essay, written, as it is, by a brand saved from the burning. Mr. Zitali was for a long time in the employ of Messrs. Mañanâ, the restaurant keepers, and no one is better fitted to deal strenuously with the awful problems of our great cities.

Manning Green is about to disappear, and all its wonderful associations will become (in the words of Swinburne)

"Smoke, or the smoke of a smoke."

But until it disappears, and until its purchase price is finally fixed by the committee, its historical associations will still remain dear to those who (like the present writer) are interested in this corner of the Motherland. That men of our blood, and men speaking our tongue—nay, that those neither of our blood, nor speaking our tongue, but devoted to a common empire—will remember Manning Green when the sale is effected, is the passionate and heartfelt prayer of JAMES BAYLEY.

ON EDITING.

ON EDITING.

I COME now to that part of my subject where pure literature is of less moment than organization and the power of arrangement; and the last two divisions of my great task concern work which has been written by others, and with which the journalist has to deal in the capacity of manager rather than that of author. These are, a few notes upon editing, and some further remarks upon Revelations, that is, unexpected and more or less secret political announcements.

I deal here first with editing, by which I do not mean the management of a whole newspaper—for this has no connection whatever with the art of letters—but the selection, arrangement, and annotating of work produced by another hand, and entrusted to the journalist for publication in his columns. The work is far easier than might appear at first sight.

The first rule in connection with it is to offend as little as possible, and especially to spare the living.

The second rule is to cut down the matter to fit the space at your disposal. With the exception of

K—2

a number of MSS. so small that they may be neglected in the calculation, it does not matter in the least what you cut out, so long as you remember that the parts remaining must make sense, and so long as you make this second rule fit in with the exigencies of the first.

As for annotation, it is the easiest thing in the world. True to the general principle which governs all good journalism, that the giving of pleasure should always be preferred to the giving of pain, let your annotations pleasantly recall to the reader his own stock of knowledge, let them be as obvious as possible, and let him not learn too much from your research. This method has the additional advantage, that it also saves you an infinity of trouble.

The matter is really not so elaborate as to need any further comment. I will proceed at once to my example, prefacing it only with the shortest explanatory statement, which will show how thoroughly it illustrates the rules I have just enunciated.

The wife of one of the principal candidates for Parliament in our part of the country begged Dr. Caliban to publish a simple, chatty diary, which her sister (who was married to a neighbouring squire) had kept during some years. Dr. Caliban was too courteous to refuse, and had too profound an acquaintance with the rural character to despise this kind of copy. On the other hand, he was compelled to point out that he could not allow the series to run through more than six months, and that he should, therefore, be compelled to cut it down at his discretion. Full leave was given him, and I do not think any man could have done the work better.

Thus the lady's husband, though a good Englishman in every other way (an indulgent landlord and a sterling patriot), was German by birth and language. Here was a truth upon which it would have been uncharitable and useless to insist—a truth which it was impossible to conceal, but which it was easy to glide over; and Dr. Caliban, as the student will see in a moment, glode over it with the lightest of feet.

Again, a very terrible tragedy had taken place in the Burpham family, and is naturally alluded to by their near neighbour. It was impossible to cut out all mention of this unhappy thing, without destroying the diary; but in Dr. Caliban's edition of the MS., the whole is left as vague as may be.

The particular part which I have chosen for a model—I think the most admirable piece of editing I know—is from that week of the diary which concerns the outbreak of the recent difficulty with France, a difficulty luckily immediately arranged, after scarcely a shot had been fired, by the mutual assent of the two nations and (as it is whispered) by the direct intervention of High Authority.

The motto which Dr. Caliban chose for the whole series (called, by the way, "Leaves from a Country Diary"), is a fine sentence from the works of Mr. Bagehot.

LEAVES FROM A COUNTRY DIARY.

"An aristocratic body firmly rooted in the national soil is not only the permanent guarantee of the security of the State, but resembles, as it were, a man better instructed than his fellows—more prompt, possessed of ample means, and yet entrusted with power: a man moreover who never dies."

February 2nd, 19—.—To-day is the Purification. The lawn looked lovely under its veil of snow, and the vicar came in to lunch. We did not discuss the question of the service, because I know that Reuben disapproves of it. The vicar told me that Mrs. Burpham is in dreadful trouble. It seems that the Bank at Molesworth refused to cash Algernon's cheque, and that this led Sir Henry Murling to make investigations about the Chattington affair, so that he had to be asked to resign his commission. To be sure it is only in the Militia, but if it all comes out, it will be terrible for the Monsons. They have already had to dismiss two servants on these grounds. Jane has a sore throat, and I made her gargle some turpentine and oil; Ali Baba's* hock is still sore. I do hope I shall keep my old servants, it is an unwelcome thing to dismiss them in their old age and the house is never the same again. They meet to-morrow at Gumpton corner, but not if this weather holds.

February 3rd, 19—.—It is thawing. There are marks of boots across the lawn on what is left of the snow, and I am afraid some one must have gone across it. I wish Reuben would come back. Called

* The pet name of the white pony. The name is taken from the *Arabian Nights*.

at Mrs. Burpham's, who is in dreadful trouble. Algernon has gone up to town to see his solicitor. Poor Mrs. Burpham was crying; she is so proud of her boy. He says it will be all right. They are very bitter against the Bank, and Sir Henry, and the regiment, and the Monsons. I fear they may quarrel with Binston Park* also. Mrs. Burpham was so curious about them; Jane is no better.

February 4th, 19—.—Reuben came home suddenly by the 2.40 with Mr. Ehrenbreitstein and Lord Tenterworth. He asked me to put Mr. Ehrenbreitstein in the Blue room and Lord Tenterworth in the Parrot room opposite the broom and pail place, where Aunt Marjory used to sleep. I shall have to clear the clothes out of the drawers. Just before dinner Mr. Bischoffen came in from the station. Reuben told me he had asked him. I wish he would give me longer notice. He brought a secretary with him who cannot talk English. I think he must be a Spaniard—he is so dark. Jane can hardly speak, her throat is so bad; I told her she might stay in bed to-morrow till nine.

February 5th, 19—.—Mrs. Burpham is certainly in dreadful trouble. She tells me Algernon has written from St. Malo saying it will be all right. It was very foolish and imprudent of him to go over there just

* The use of the name of an estate in the place of the name of its owner or owners is very common with the territorial class in our countrysides. Thus, people will say, "I have been calling at the Laurels," or "I dined with the Monkey Tree"; meaning, "I have been calling upon Mrs. So-and-So," or, "I have been dining with Sir Charles Gibbs."

now with all this trouble on with France. If only he had stayed at home (Mrs. Burpham says) she would not have minded so much, but she is afraid of his getting killed. It seems they are so savage at St. Malo.* Only the other day an English lady had a stone thrown in her direction in the street. Mr. Bischoffen's secretary is not a Spaniard; I think he is a Pole; his name is Brahms. There was a difficulty about the asparagus last night. It seems the Germans do not eat it with their fingers. Reuben said I ought to have got little silver pincers for it. I remember seeing them in his father's house, but papa said they were very vulgar. *Then* Reuben used to apologise for them, and say that his people were old fashioned, which was nonsense, of course. I reminded Reuben of this, and he said, "Ach! Gott!" and I had to leave the room. Ali Baba is all right; he took a piece of sugar from my hand; but when I felt his hock he kicked Jones severely. I fear Jones is really injured, and I have sent for Dr. Minton and for the veterinary surgeon.

February 6th, 19—.—Dr. Minton dined here last night before going to set Jones' leg, and I gave the veterinary surgeon supper in the old schoolroom. I am afraid Dr. Minton took too much wine, for he quarrelled with Mr. Ehrenbreitstein and Mr. Bischoffen about the danger of war with France. He said they had no right to speak, and got quite excited. Called again on Mrs. Burpham, and only appreciated fully to-day in what sad trouble she is. Algernon has

* A seaport in Britanny.

telegraphed from Paris saying it will be all right. Meanwhile she has certainly quarrelled with Binston Park, and she even spoke bitterly against the Duke, so that means another family gone—for the Duke is very proud. I see in the *Standard* that our Ambassador has delivered an ultimatum, and that the French are doing all they can to shirk war. That is what Mr. Bischoffen and Reuben said they would do, but they must be taught a lesson. Newfoundlands have fallen, but Reuben says they must rise after the war. I do hope they will. The dear Bishop called. He says this war is a judgment on the French. Jane is much better, and can talk quite clearly, and Ali Baba is almost well. Also it has thawed now completely, and they can meet on Saturday as usual, so things are looking up all round.

February 7th, 19—.—Freddie goes to the Isle of Wight with the Lambtonshire Regiment, and Mrs. Burpham and the Bishop are both delighted, because it will bring him and Hepworth together. It would be such a solace to poor Mrs. Burpham if Freddie could see active service and get promotion; it would help to wipe out Algernon's disgrace, for I fear there is now no doubt of it, though he says it is all right in his last letter, which is from Marseilles. Letters still come through from France, because our Ambassador said that if any tricks were played with them he would hold the French Government personally responsible, and so cowed them. The Bishop has gone to London with his family.

February 8th, 19—.—The *Standard* has a large map of

the North of France, where the fighting will be. It is very interesting. Reuben and his friends have gone up to town again. I saw the Reserves marching through Molesworth to-day; they are going to garrison Portsmouth.* The afternoon post did not come in. Reuben said he would telegraph, but I have not got any message. The 12.40 train was an hour late, so I suppose everything is upset by the war. Maria will have to come home by Bâle, and I do so dread the passage from Ostend for her; even the hour from Calais to Dover is more than she can bear. The vicar says that our Government will force the French to keep the Dover-Calais route open for civilians. He says it would be against the practice of civilised warfare to close it, and if that were done we should lay waste the whole country; but I fear he does not know much about the legal aspect of the thing: it is his heart, not his head that speaks. It is dreadful to think what I shall do with Mademoiselle† when she comes home with Maria. One can't blame her when one thinks that it is her own country that is going to be harried and her own brothers brought here as prisoners; but it will be very difficult all the same. The man who was killed at Bigley races was not a Frenchman after all: the crowd only thought he was because he had blacked his face like a negro. It seems that Sir Henry was very hard in court, and said that the ringleaders were lucky not to be indicted

* A large military port and dockyard on the coast of Hampshire.

† The generic term among the wealthy for French menials of the weaker sex.

for manslaughter. It has frozen again, and it is very slippery in the drive. They are having fireworks or something at Portsmouth, to judge by the sound. Jones told Jane he thought there was a bonfire as well, because he could see a glare now and then in the sky from the window in his room. His leg is setting nicely.

ON REVELATIONS.

Revelations, again, as we found to be the case with editing, do not properly constitute a department of the art of letters. Though they are of far more importance than any other branch of contemporary journalism, yet it is impossible to compare their publication to a creative act of pure literature.

It may be urged that such Revelations as are written in the office of the newspaper publishing them are not only literature, but literature of a very high order. They are, on the face of it, extremely difficult to compose. If they are to have any chance of deceiving the public, the writer must thoroughly know the world which he counterfeits; he must be able to copy its literary style, its air, its errors. It is even sometimes necessary for him to attempt the exquisitely subtle art of forgery.

The objection is well found; but it is not of this kind of Revelation that I propose to speak. It belongs to the higher branches of our art, and is quite unsuited to a little elementary manual.

The Revelation I speak of here is the ordinary type of private communication, domestic treason, or accidental discovery, dealing, as a rule, with public affairs, and brought to the office spontaneously by servants, colonial adventurers, or ministers of religion.

Nine Revelations out of ten are of this kind; and the young journalist who may desire to rise in his great calling must make himself thoroughly familiar with the whole process by which they are to be procured and published.

A small amount of additional matter has, indeed, sometimes to be furnished, but it is almost insignificant, and is, moreover, of so conventional a nature, that it need not trouble us for a moment. Some such phrase as "We have received the following communication from a source upon which we place the firmest reliance," will do very well to open with, and at the end: "We shall be interested to see what reply can be given to the above," is a very useful formula. Thus the words "To be continued," added at the end are often highly lucrative. They were used by the *Courrier des Frises* (a first-class authority on such matters), when it recently published a number of private letters, written (alas!) in the English tongue, and concerning the noblest figure in English politics.

But though there is little to be done in the way of writing, there is a considerable mental strain involved in judging whether a particular Revelation will suit the proprietor of the newspaper upon which one is employed, and one must not unfrequently be prepared to suffer from exhausting terrors for some weeks after its publication.

Difficult as is the art of testing Revelation, the rules that govern it are few and simple. The Revelator, if a domestic servant, wears a round black bowler hat and a short jacket, and a pair of very good trousers stolen from his master; he will be clean shaven. If an adventurer or minister of religion, he will wear a soft felt hat and carry a large muffler round his throat. Either sort walk noiselessly, but the first in a firm, and the second in a shuffling manner. I am far from saying that all who enter newspaper offices under this appearance bear with them Revelations even of the mildest kind, but I do say that whenever Revelations come, they are brought by one of these two kinds of men.

I should add that the Revelator like the money-lender, the spy, and every other professional man whose livelihood depends upon efficiency is invariably sober. If any man come to you with a Revelation and seem even a trifle drunk, dismiss him without inquiry, though not before you have admonished him upon his shame and sin, and pointed out the ruin that such indulgence brings upon all save the wealthy.

When a man arrives who seems at all likely to have a Revelation in his pocket, and who offers it for sale, remember that you have but a few moments in which to make up your mind; put him into the little room next to the sub-editor, take his MS., tell him you will show it to your chief, and, as you leave him, lock the door softly on the outside.

The next moment may decide your whole career. You must glance at the Revelation, and judge in that glance whether the public will believe it even for two full hours. The whole difference between a successful and an unsuccessful journalist lies in that power of sudden vision; nor will experience alone achieve it, it must be experience touched with something like genius.

Libellous matter you can delete. Matter merely false will not be remembered against you; but if that rare and subtle character which convinces the mob be lacking, *that* is a thing which no one can supply in the time between the Revelator's arrival and the paper's going to press.

Finally, when you have made your decision, return, unlock, pay, and dismiss. Never pay by cheque. Remember how short is the time at your disposal. Remember that if your paper does not print a really good Revelation when it is offered, some other paper will. Remember the *Times*, the *Chronicle*, and Major Esterhazy. Remember Mr. Gladstone's resignation. . . . Remember the "Maine."

A few practical instances will help us to understand these abstract rules.

Consider, for instance, the following—one of the wisest acts of Dr. Caliban's whole life.

Dr. Caliban was busy writing a leader for the *Sunday Englishman* upon "Hell or Immortality"; for it was Saturday night, he had just received the weekly papers, and, as he well said, "A strong Sunday paper has this advantage, that it can do what it likes with the weeklies."

He was, I say in the midst of Hell or Immortality, when he was interrupted by a note. He opened it, read it, frowned, and passed it to me, saying:—

"What do you make of this?"

The note ran :—

> "I have just been dismissed from the *Spectator* for sneezing in an indelicate manner. I have a Revelation to make with regard to the conduct of that paper. Please see me at once, or it may be too late. I have with me a letter which the *Spectator* will publish next week. It throws a searching light upon the Editor's mind, and lays bare all the inner workings of the paper. Price 40s."

I told Dr. Caliban, that in my opinion, on the one hand, there might be something in it; while on the other hand, that there might not.

Dr. Caliban looked at me thoughtfully and said:

"You think that?"

He touched an electric bell. As this did not ring, he blew down a tube, and receiving no answer, nor indeed hearing the whistle at the other end, he sent a messenger, who, by some accident, failed to return to the editorial office. Dr. Caliban himself went down and brought up the stranger. He was a young man somewhat cadaverous. He repeated what he had said in his note, refused to bargain in any way, received two sovereigns from Dr. Caliban's own purse, sighed deeply, and then with a grave face said:

"It feels like treason."

He pressed his lips hard together, conquered himself, and left us with the utmost rapidity.

When Dr. Caliban and I were alone together, he opened the sealed envelope and read these words, written on a little slip of foolscap:

"*The following letter is accepted by the Spectator, and will be printed next week.*" To this slip was pinned a rather dirty half sheet of note paper, and on this was the following letter:

Balcarry Castle,
County Mayo.
Jan. 19th, 1903.

To the Editor of the *Spectator*.

Dear Sir,

Among your humorous Irish stories perhaps the following will be worthy to find a place. A dear uncle of mine, my father's half brother, and the husband of the talented E. J. S., was bishop of Killibardine, a prelate of great distinction and considerable humour.

I well remember that somewhere in the summer of 1869, his valet having occasion to call unexpectedly upon a relative (butler to the Duke of Kerry), the latter observed "Indade, an' shure now an' is that yourself, Pat, Pat asthor, at all, at all," to which the witty fellow answered, with the true Irish twinkle in his eye, "Was your grandfather a monkey?"

I am very faithfully yours,
THE MACFFIN.

Dr. Caliban was heartily amused by the tale, and told me that he had met the MacFfin some years ago at Lady Marroway's.

"Nevertheless," he added, I don't think it would be fair to comment on the little story . . . I had imagined that something graver was toward . . "

He never spoke again of the small outlay he had made, and I afterwards found that it had been included in the general expenses of the paper. I have never forgotten the lesson, nor since that date have I ever accepted MSS. and paid for it without making myself acquainted to some extent with the subject. A little such foresight upon that occasion would have convinced us that a letter of this kind would never have found a place in a review of the calibre of the *Spectator.*

Contrast with Dr. Caliban's wise and patriotic conduct upon this occasion the wickedness and folly of the *Evening German* in the matter of the Cabinet Crisis.

For some time the saner papers, which see the Empire as it is, had been issuing such placards as "He must go," "Make room for Joseph" and other terse and definite indications of a new policy.

The *Evening German* had for several days headed its leading article, "Why don't he resign?"

A member of the unscrupulous gang who ever lie in wait for whatever is innocent and enthusiastic called, just before press, upon the editor of the *Evening German*, passing himself off as the valet of the minister whose resignation was demanded. He produced a small sheet of MSS., and affirmed it to be the exact account of an interview between the minister and his doctor, which interview the valet had overheard, "concealed," as he put it "behind an arras." He said it would explain the situation thoroughly. He received no less than 25 guineas, and departed.

Now let the student read what follows, and ask himself by what madness a responsible editor came to print a thing so self-evidently absurd.

WHY HE DOES NOT RESIGN!

We have received upon an unimpeachable authority the verbatim account of an interview between him and his medical adviser, which we think thoroughly explains the present deadlock in Imperial affairs. We are assured upon oath that he was in bed when the doctor called just before noon yesterday, and that the following dialogue took place:—

MINISTER (*in bed*)—Good morning, Doctor, I am glad to see you. What can I do for you? . . . I mean, I am glad to see you. Pray excuse the inadvertence of my phrase, it is one that I have lately had to use not a little.

DOCTOR—Pray let me look at your tongue and feel your pulse. So. We are getting along nicely. At what hour were you thinking of rising?

MINISTER—At twelve, my usual hour. I see no reason for lying in bed, Doctor. (*There was a despairing tone in this phrase*). I am well enough, Doctor, well enough. (*Here he gazed sadly out of the window into St. James's Park*). I am a Minister, but I cannot minister to a mind diseased (*this rather bitterly*). There is nothing the matter with me.

DOCTOR (*cheerily*)—My dear Mr. ——, do not talk so. You will be spared many, many useful years, I hope. Indeed, I am sure. There is, as you say, nothing the matter—nothing organically the matter; this lassitude and nervous exhaustion from which you suffer is a distressing, but a common symptom of mental activity. (*Here the doctor dived into a black bag*). Let me sound the chest.

MINISTER—Will it hurt? (*This was said rather anxiously*).

DOCTOR—Not a bit of it. I only wish to make assurance doubly sure—as we say in the profession. (*He put the stethoscope to the chest of the Cabinet Minister*). Now draw a deep breath . . . no, deeper than that . . . a really deep breath.

MINISTER (*gasping*)—I can't.

DOCTOR—Tut, tut. . . . Well, it's all a question of lungs. (*Here he moved the stethoscope again*). Now sing.

MINISTER—La! La! . . . La!

DOCTOR—Nothing wrong with the lungs. Only a little feeble perhaps. Do you take any exercise?

MINISTER (*wearily*)—Oh! yes . . . I walk about. . . . I used to walk a lot in Ireland. . . . I'm not like Ch——n; he never takes any exercise (*bitterly*); but then, he was brought up differently. (*Sadly*) Oh Doctor! I am so tired! . . . My back aches.

DOCTOR—Well, Mr. ——, a little rest will do you all the good in the world. You have the Easter recess in which to take a thorough rest. Do not lie in bed all day; get up about five and drive to your club. Whatever you do, don't write or think, and don't let them worry you with callers. (*The Doctor here prepared to leave*).

MINISTER (*hopelessly*)—Doctor . . . there is something I want to ask you. . . . *Can't* I give it up?

Doctor (*firmly*)—No, Mr. ——, no. Upon no account. I have told your uncle and your cousins so fifty times. It is a point upon which I must be firm. Politics are a necessity to you all. I would not answer for you if it were not for politics. (*Sympathetically*) You are none of you strong.

Minister (*heaving a deep sigh*)—No. I am not strong. . . . Alas! . . . . Chaplin is. But then, Chaplin's built differently. . . . I wish you would let me give it up, Doctor?

Doctor (*kindly*)—No, my dear Mr. ——, *No!* Pray put such thoughts out of your head. Every man must occupy his brain and body. Most men discover or choose an occupation, but I have not been a family doctor for thirty years without distinguishing these from such rare organisms as yours—and your family's. The House of Commons is the saving of you. (*The Doctor here paused, gazed anxiously at Mr. ——, and said slowly*) Perhaps, though, you take your work too seriously. It is often so with highly strung men. Do as little as you can.

Minister—I do . . . but still it wearies me inexpressibly.

Doctor—Not so much as writing a book would, or travel, or country walks.

Minister (*shaking his head*)—I never felt so tired after "It May be True," nor even after "I Greatly Doubt It," as I do now (*smiling a little*). They sold well.

Doctor—And why? Because you were engaged in politics. Believe me, dear Mr. ——, without that one regular employment you would do little or nothing. It is the balance-wheel that regulates your whole system. Change the rules, and, if you will, limit debate to a minimum, but do not think of giving up the one thing that keeps up your circulation. More men die from inanition than I care to tell you.

MINISTER—Very well, Doctor . . . (*weakly and quietly*) it is nearly one; I must sleep . . . Good-bye.

The Doctor here went out on tip-toe. The Minister slept. There was a great silence.

The *Evening German* suffered severely, and would have been ruined but for the prompt action of the Frankfort House; and the whole incident shows as clearly as possible what perils surround the most tempting, but the most speculative, sort of journalistic enterprise.

The student may tell me—and justly—that I have offered him none but negative examples. I will complete his instruction by printing one of the best chosen Revelations I know.

At the time when a number of letters addressed to Mr. Kruger by various public men were captured, and very rightly published, a certain number were, for reasons of State, suppressed. To Dr. Caliban, reasons of State were no reasons; he held that no servant of the people had a right to keep the people in ignorance.

Within a week, a detective in his employ had brought a little sheaf of documents, which, judged by internal evidence alone, were plainly genuine.

They were printed at once. They have never since been challenged.

I.

497, Jubilee Row,
B'ham,
19.7.'99.

Dear Sir.—We must respectfully press for the payment of our account. The terms upon which the ammunition was furnished were strictly cash, and, as you will see by the terms of our letter of the 15th last, we cannot tolerate any further delay. If we do not hear from you relative to same by next mail, we shall be compelled to put the matter into the hands of our solicitors.

Yours, &c.,
John Standfast,
Pro Karl Biffenheimer and Co.

II.

Yacht *Fleur de Lys.*
Prince de Vaigne.

Palerme,
Sicile.
Ci, la feste de l'Assomption de la T.S.V.
(Vieux Style)
L'an de N.S.J.C. MCM.
(1900).

Monsieur Mon Frère.—Nous vous envoyons nos remerciemens pour vos souhaits et vous assurons de la parfaicte amictié qui liera toujours nos couronnes alliées. Faictes. Continuez.

Agréez, Monsieur Mon Frère, l'assurance de notre consideration Royale la plus distinguée.

ORLÉANS,
pour le Roy,
Chétif.

Vu, pour copie conforme,
Le Seneschal, BRU.

III.

Offices of the *Siècle*,
Paris,
Chef-lieu of the
department of the Seine,
France.
6, Thermidor, 108.

My good Kruger.—It is evidently necessary that I should speak out to you in plain English. I can't go into a long dissertation, but if you will read the books I send herewith, *The Origin of Species*, Spencer's *Sociology*, Grant Allen's *Evolution of the Idea of God*, &c., you will see why I can't back you up. As for your contemptible offer, I cast it back at you with disdain. My name alone should have protected me from such insults. I would have you know that my paper represents French opinion in England, and is now owned by an international company. I am the irremovable editor.

Yours with reserve,
YVES GUYOT.

P.S.—I have been a Cabinet Minister. I send you a circular of our new company. It is a good thing. Push it along.

IV.

The Chaplaincy,
Barford College,
Old St. Winifred's Day,
1900.

My dear Mr. Kruger.—Your position is at once interesting and peculiar, and deserves, as you say, my fullest attention. On the one hand (as you well remark) you believe you have a right to your independence, and that our Government has no moral right to interfere in your domestic affairs. You speak warmly of Mr. Chamberlain and describe him as lacking in common morality or (as we put it) in breeding. I think you are hardly fair. Mr. Chamberlain has his own morality, and in that summing up of all ethics which we in England call "manners," he is indistinguishable from other gentlemen of our class. He has had a great deal to bear and he has latterly borne it in silence. It is hardly the part of a generous foe to taunt him now. I fear you look upon these matters a little narrowly and tend to accept one aspect as the absolute. The truth is that international morality must always be largely Utilitarian, and in a very interesting little book by Beeker it is even doubted whether what we call "ethics" have any independent existence. This new attitude (which we call "moral anarchism") has lately cast a great hold upon our younger men and is full of interesting possibilities.

If you meet Milner you should discuss the point with him. I assure you this school is rapidly ousting the old "comparative-positive" in which he and Curzon were trained. There is a great deal of self-realization going on also. Lord Mestenvaux (whom you have doubtless met—he was a director of the Johannesberg Alcohol Concession) is of my opinion.

Believe me, my dear Mr. Kruger, with the fullest and warmest sympathy for such of your grievances as may be legitimate, and with the ardent prayer that the result of this deplorable quarrel may turn out to be the best for *both* parties,

Your affectionate Friend of old days,

JOSHIA LAMBKIN, M.A.,

Fellow and Chaplain.

V.

(Telegram.)

Send orders payable Amsterdam immediate, Liberal party clamouring . . . (name illegible) risen to ten thousand, market firm and rising. Waste no money on comic paper. Not Read.

(Unsigned.)

Finally this damning piece of evidence must close the terrible series.

VI.

To the Rev. Ebenezer Biggs, Capetown.

The House of Commons,

April 10th, 1899.

My dear Sir.—You put me in a very difficult position, for, on the one hand, I cannot, and would not, work against the interests of my country, and, on the other hand, I am convinced that Mr. Chamberlain is determined to plunge that country into the war spoken of by John in Revelations ix. Anything I can do for peace I will, but for some reason or other the *Times* will not insert my letters, though I write to them twice and sometimes thrice in one day. Sir Alfred Milner was once very rude to me. He is a weak man morally, mainly intent upon "getting on;" he has agreed since his youth with every single person of influence (except myself) whom he happened to come across, and is universally liked. I fear that no one's private influence can do much. The London Press has been bought in a lump by two financiers. Perhaps a little waiting is the best thing. There is sure to be a reaction, and after all, Mr. Chamberlain is a man of a very low order. His mind, I take it, is not unlike his face. He thinks very little and very clearly . . . I have really nothing more to say.

Always your sincere friend,

EDWARD BAYTON.

No one knew better than Dr. Caliban that a Revelation is but weakened by comment. But the war was at its height, and he could not read without disgust such words, written in such a place by such a man.

He added the note:

"We understand that the law officers of the Crown are debating whether or no the concluding sentences of this disgraceful letter can be made to come within 26 Edward III., cap. 37, defining high treason. It is

> certainly not a physical attack upon the Person, Consort, or offspring of the Crown, nor is it (strictly speaking) giving aid to the Queen's enemies. On the other hand, it is devoutly hoped that the attack on Mr. Chamberlain can be made to fall under 32 Henry VIII., 1, whereby it is felony to strike or 'provoke' the King's servants within the precincts of the Palace. The infamous screed was certainly written in a palace, and Mr. Chamberlain is as certainly a servant of the Queen. He certainly was provoked—nay nettled. The latter clauses of the act, condemning those who attack the doctrine of Transubstantiation to be roasted alive, have, of course, fallen into desuetude. The earlier, milder, and more general clauses stand, and *should be enforced.*"

Let me not be misunderstood. I think it was an error to pen that comment. Strong expressions, used in a time of high party feeling, may look exaggerated when they survive into quieter times. But if it was an error, it was the only error that can be laid to the charge of a just and great man in the whole course of forty years, during which period he occasionally edited as many as five journals at a time.

SPECIAL PROSE.

SPECIAL PROSE.

Mrs. Caliban begged me to add a few words on "Special Prose," and to subjoin an example of that manner. She has suggested for the latter purpose Mrs. Railston's "Appreciation of William Shakespeare," written as a preface for the Charing Cross Shakespeare in 1897. She has even been at the pains of asking Mrs. Railston's leave to have it included in this volume, a permission that was at once granted, accompanied with the courteous request that Mrs. Railston's name, address, and private advertisement should accompany the same.

Were I dependent upon my own judgment alone, the wisdom of adding such a division at the close of these essays might seem doubtful. Special Prose is an advanced kind of literature, too great an attraction to which might at first confuse rather than aid the student; and I should hardly make a place for it in a straightforward little Text-book.

Mrs. Caliban's wishes in all matters concerning this work must be observed, and I have done what she desired me, even to the degree of printing Mrs. Railston's advertisement, though I am certain that great Authoress does herself harm by this kind of insistence . . . It is no business of mine. . . .

M—2

It is only fair to add that prose of this sort *is* the highest form of our Art, and should be the ultimate goal of every reader of this Guide. If, however, the student is bewildered in his first attempt to decipher it (as he very well may be), my advice to him is this: let him mark the point to which he has persevered, and then put the whole thing aside until he has had some little further practice in English letters. Then let him return, fresh from other work, some weeks later, and see if he cannot penetrate still further into the close-knit texture. Soon he will find it almost like his own tongue, and will begin to love and to understand.

Not many months will pass before it will mean to him something more than life, as he once imagined, could contain.

Having said so much, let me hasten to obey Mrs. Caliban's command.

WILLIAM SHAKESPEARE.

An Appreciation.

BY MARGARET RAILSTON.

How very manifestly well did not Montaigne (I think it was) say in his essay upon Value that the "inner part of Poesy is whilom hid, whilom bare, and it matters little whether it be bare or hidden." That was a sentence such as our Wordsworth might have quoted at the high court of Plato when the poets were arraigned as unworthy to be rooted in his Republic. For the most part these dear poets of our tongue will rather have it bare than hidden, leaving the subtleties of "The Misanthrope" to another race, and themselves preferring the straight verbal stab of "The Idiot Boy" or "Danny Deever;" so that many of us see nothing in the Rhymed Heroics of the Grand Siècle. Yet Molière also had genius.

"Molière a du génie et Christian été beau."

That sentence given nasally by a Coquelin to a theatre-full of People of the Middle-Class should convince also us of the Hither-North that flowers may blow in any season and be as various as multiplicity may.

William Shakespeare, without all question and beyond any repining, is—or rather was—the first of our Poets, and was—or rather is—the first to-day. So that, with him for a well and the Jacobean Bible for a further spring of effort, our English Poets make up ("build" Milton called it) the sounding line. But William Shakespeare also is of us: he will have it on the surface or not at all; as a man hastening to beauty, too eager to delve by the way. And with it all how he succeeds! What grace and what appreciation in epithet, what subtle and sub-conscious effects of verb! What resonant and yet elusive diction! It is true Shakespeare, that line—

"Rough winds do shake the darling buds of May."

And that other—

"Or stoops with the Remover to remove."

And these are true Shakespeare because in each there

is we know not what of ivory shod with steel. A mixture of the light and the strong, of the subtle and the intense rescues his simple words from oblivion. But another, not of our blood, would have hidden far more; he shows it all, frankly disdaining artifice.

Also the great Elizabethan needs room for his giant limbs, for his frame of thought and his thews of diction. Cite him just too shortly, choose but a hair's breadth too mickle an ensample of his work, and it is hardly Poesy, nay, hardly Prose. Thus you shall have Othello—the Moor they call him—betrayed and raging, full of an African Anger. What does he say of it? Why very much; but if you are of those that cut out their cameos too finely; you slip into quoting this merely:—

Oth. Hum! Hum!

And that is not our Shakespeare at all, nor e'en our Othello. Oh! no, it is nothing but a brutish noise, meaning nothing, empty of tragedy, unwished for.

It was Professor Goodle who said that "none needed the spaces of repose more than Shakespeare," and taught us in these words that the poet must have hills and valleys; must recline if he is to rise. But does not Shakespeare, even in his repose, seem to create? The Professor will indeed quote to us the mere sprawling leisure of Stratford, and shame us with such lines as—

MAC.—The Devil damn thee black, thou cream-faced loon,
Where got'st thou that goose look?

Which is Shakespeare at full length. But we also, that are not over sure of Shakespeare's failing, can answer him with such excerpts as these :—

> HEN.—Therefore do thou, stiff-set Northumberland,
> Retire to Chester, and my cousin here,
> The noble Bedford, hie to Glo'ster straight
> And give our Royal ordinance and word
> That in this fit and strife of empery
> No loss shall stand account. To this compulsion
> I pledge my sword, my person and my honour
> On the Great Seal of England : so farewell.
> Swift to your charges : nought was ever done
> Unless at some time it were first begun.

This also is Shakespeare in his repose, but a better Shakespeare than he whom the Professor would challenge. For though there is here no work or strain in the thing, yet it reeks of English. It is like the mist over our valleys at evening, so effortless is it and so reposeful, and yet so native. Note the climax "On the Great Seal of England" and the quaint, characteristic folklore of the concluding couplet, with its rhyming effect. Note also how sparing is William Shakespeare of the strong qualificative, however just it may be. For when our moderns will speak hardly of "the tolerant kine" or "the under-lit sky," or of "the creeping river like a worm upturned, with silver belly stiffened in the grass," though they be by all this infinitely stronger, yet are they but the more condensed and self-belittled. Shakespeare will write you ten lines and have in all but one just and sharp adjective—"stiff-set;" for the rest they are a common highway ; he cares not.

And here he is in the by-paths; a meadow of

Poesy. I have found it hidden away in one of the latter plays; the flowers of his decline :—

> "Fear no more the heat o' the sun,
> Nor the furious winter's rages;
> Now thine earthly task is done,
> Thou'rt gone home and ta'en thy wages.
> Golden lads and lasses must,
> Like chimney-sweepers, come to dust."

There is in that a line I swear no one but Shakespeare would have dared. "Thou'rt gone home and ta'en thy wages." Commonplace? A text on the wall? A sermon-tag? All you will, but a *frame for glory*.

This then is William Shakespeare in a last word. A man at work full of doing; the Fἔργον: glad if you saw the mark of the chisel; still more glad if you did not see it. And if it be queried why are such things written of him? Why do we of the last and woful days turn and return the matter of our past? We say this. *Vixere Fortes;* that is, no fame were enduring save by continued iterance and echo of similar praise, nor any life well earned in the public sheets that dared not touch on any matter and remodel all. It is for ourselves and for William Shakespeare that these things are done. For ourselves, that is a private thing to hide under the veil of the Home-lofe. For William Shakespeare, that is the public duty, that his fame may not fail in the noise of new voices. And we can borrow from him and return to him what he said of another with such distinction of plane and delicate observance of value :—

> "So long as men shall breathe and eyes can see,
> This lives, and living, this gives life to thee."

[Notices in this manner can be furnished at reasonable notice upon any poet, preferably a young or a modern poet, on the usual terms. The style is produced in seven distinct sizes, of which this is No. 3. Please state No. when ordering. All envelopes to be addressed.

Mrs. Margaret Railston,
c/o Charlie Bernberg,
48, Upper Gannimore Gardens,
Shepherd's Bush, W.

All envelopes to be marked "Appreciation." Accounts monthly. All cheques to be crossed "Becker, Becker, & Bernberg."]

PRICES CURRENT.

In all ordinary lines Prices were well maintained and rising at the outbreak of the Spanish-American War. They rose sharply thenceforward till the second week of the war in South Africa, since which date they have been sagging, touching bed rock in the spring of this year (March, 1903). There has been a slight reaction since the beginning of the season, but it is not supported, and the market is still extremely dull. Patriotic Poems have fallen out of sight, and Criticism is going begging: in some offices books are no longer given to their reviewers: sub-editors have latterly been asked to bring their own suppers. The pinch is being felt everywhere. Police reports are on piece-work and the Religious Column is shut down to half shifts. Leader writers have broken from 1100 a year to 300. Editors have suffered an all-round cut in wages of 25 per cent. Publishers' carrying-over days are more anxious than ever. Several first-class houses were hammered on the last contango, and the Banks are calling in loans. Private capital can hardly be obtained save for day-to-day transactions, and even so at very high rates of interest. The only lines that are well maintained are City Articles and Special Prose. Snippets are steady.

The following list is taken from Hunter's Handbook, and represents Prices at the close of May:—

PROSE.

(*Prices in shillings per thousand words*).

			Rise or Fall.
Special Prose	30/-	35/-	Unchanged.
Street Accidents	10/-	12/-	— 5/-
Reviews	7/6	10/-	—20/-
Police Court Notices ...	15/-	18/-	— 5/-
Guaranteed Libels ...	25/-	30/-	— 3/-
Unguaranteed ditto ...	5/-	7/-	+ 2/-
Deferred ditto	14/-	16/-	+ 4/-
Pompous Leaders ...	8/-	10/-	—25/- !
Smart Leaders	9/-	11/6	+ 3/-
Ten-line Leaderettes ...	10/-	12/-	Unchanged.
Political Appeals ...	15/-	17/-	—30/-
Attacks on Foreign Nations	3/-	3/6	—48/- !!
Dramatic Criticism ...	20/-	25/-	Unchanged.
Historical Work	—	6d. ?	(Practically no demand).
Religious Notes	12/-	18/-	— 8/-
Attacks upon Christianity	4/-	4/6	— 5/- (A very heavy fall for this kind of matter).

VERSE.

(*Prices in pence per line*).

Bad Verse ... No price can be given—very variable.
Good minor Verse. 3d. (much the same as last year).
Special Verse ... 1/- (a heavy fall).

READY RECKONER.

This Table does not profess any minute accuracy; it will, however, be found amply sufficient for all practical purposes.

Pence per Line.	Shillings per Long Column.			Shillings per Short Column.			Pounds per Thousand Words.
	Pica.	Bourgeois.	Minion.*	Pica.	Bourgeois.	Minion.*	
$\frac{1}{4}$*d.*	3/9	4/3	5/-	3/-	3/9	4/6	†£0·16378.
$\frac{1}{2}$*d.*	7/6	8/6	10/-	6/-	7/6	9/-	£0·32757.
$\frac{3}{4}$*d.*	11/3	12/9	15/-	9/-	11/3	13/6	£0·49135.
‡1*d.*	15/-	17/-	20/-	12/-	15/-	18/-	£0·65514.
1$\frac{1}{2}$*d.*	22/6	25/6	30/-	18/-	22/6	27/-	£0·98270.¶
§2*d.*	30/-	34/-	40/-	24/-	30/-	36/-	£1·31028.
2$\frac{1}{2}$*d.*	37/6	42/6	50/-	30/-	37/6	45/-	£1·63705.

No prices superior to this last for Prose.

Verse up to 1/- a line. See preceding page, not reckoned in cols. or 1000 words.

* Always allow minion for extracts and quotations.

† The student must be careful in calculations involving the decimal point to put it in its exact place, neither too much to the right nor too much to the left.

‡ This may be taken as the *normal price* paid for Literature; the other prices must be compared with it as a standard.

§ No prices beyond this, save on first-class papers—the *Spectator*, *Daily Mail*, and one or two others.

¶ Practically one Pound.

(The Sections dealing with "THE DETECTION OF CLASSICAL AUTHORS" and "THE VIVID PRESENTATION OF HISTORY," have been omitted by request of the Family. It is perhaps as well.)

NOTE ON TITLES.

THE young journalist will never make an error as to the title of an individual, and his proper style and address, if he will but learn to trust the books of reference provided by the office.

They are far more accurate than other works of the kind.* Contrast, for instance, Bowley's *Peerage and Baronetage* with Bowley's *Register of Events during the past year.*

What may be called "derivative titles" differ in the most complicated manner according to the rank of the parent. It would be quite impossible for the journalist to attempt to learn them. He had far better write plain "Lord" and "Lady" where he has occasion to, and on all other occasions whatsoever, "Mr." or, if he prefer the term, "Esquire." In conversation no Lord should be addressed as "My Lord," but a Bishop should always be so addressed; no Duke should be called "Your Grace" to his face, but it is courteous to bestow this honour upon an Archbishop. It is still more important to avoid the term "milady" in speaking to the consorts

* They are often inaccurate with regard to the past history of the families mentioned, and very often wrong in the spelling of the family name; but these details are furnished by the families themselves, upon whom the responsibility must rest.

of the above named, especially in the case of bishops' wives, to whom the title does not apply. Baronets, on the other hand, must always be addressed as "Sir," followed by a Christian name. The omission to do this has led to grievous trouble. The principal English titles are, Prince, Duke, Marquis, Marquess (a more recent creation), Earl, Baron; then comes a division; then Irish Peers, Baronets, Knights, and finally Members of the Victorian Order.

The principal foreign titles are Count, Viscount (which by the way is also an English title, but I forgot it), Vidame, Chevalier, Excellency, Graf, Furst, Margrave, Baron, Boyar, Monsignor, and Grandee—the latter used only in Spain, Ceuta, and the other Spanish dominions beyond the seas.

Imperial titles are:—the Maharajah, the Maharanee, the Akon of Swat, the Meresala of Baghirmi, the Oyo of Oya, the Allemami of Foutazallam, the Ameer, the Emir, the Bally-o-Gum of Abe-o-Kuta,* and others too numerous to mention. All these should, in general, be addressed as Your Highness.

Colonials are called "The Honourable."

* I omit the ex-Jumbi of Koto-Koto, a rebellious upstart whom the Imperial Government has very properly deposed.

NOTE ON STYLE.

ONE does well to have by one a few jottings that will enable one to add to one's compositions what one call's style in case it is demanded of one by an editor.

I would not insist too much upon the point; it is simple enough, and the necessity of which I speak does not often crop up. But editors differ very much among themselves, and every now and then one gets a manuscript returned with the note, "please improve style," in blue pencil, on the margin. If one had no idea as to the meaning of this a good deal of time might be wasted, so I will add here what are considered to be the five principal canons of style or good English.

The first canon, of course, is that style should have *Distinction*. Distinction is a quality much easier to attain than it looks. It consists, on the face of it, in the selection of peculiar words and their arrangement in an odd and perplexing order, and the objection is commonly raised that such irregularities cannot be rapidly acquired. Thus the Chaplain of Barford, preaching upon style last Holy Week, remarked "there is a natural tendency in stating some useless and empty thing to express oneself in a common or vulgar manner." That is quite true, but it is a tendency which can easily be corrected, and I think that that sentence I have just quoted throws a flood of light on the reverend gentleman's own deficiencies.

Of course no writer is expected to write or even to speak in this astonishing fashion, but what is easier than to go over one's work and strike out ordinary words? There should be no hesitation as to what to put in their place. Halliwell's "Dictionary of Archaic and Provincial Words" will give one all the material one may require. Thus "lettick" is charming Rutlandshire for "decayed" or "putrescent," and "swinking" is a very good alternative for "working." It is found in Piers Plowman.

It is very easy to draw up a list of such unusual words, each corresponding with some ordinary one, and to pin it up where it will meet your eye. In all this matter prose follows very much the same rules as were discovered and laid down for verse on page 86.

The second canon of style is that it should be *obscure*, universally and without exception. The disturbance of the natural order of words to which I have just alluded is a great aid, but it is not by any means the only way to achieve the result. One should also on occasion use several negatives one after the other, and the sly correction of punctuation is very useful. I have known a fortune to be made by the omission of a full stop, and a comma put right in between a noun and its adjective was the beginning of Daniel Witton's reputation. A foreign word misspelt is also very useful. Still more useful is some allusion to some unimportant historical person or event of which your reader cannot possibly have heard.

As to the practice, which has recently grown up, of writing only when one is drunk, or of introducing plain lies into every sentence, they are quite unworthy of the stylist properly so called, and can never permanently add to one's reputation.

The third canon of style is the *occasional omission* of a verb or of the predicate. Nothing is more agreeably surprising, and nothing more effective. I have known an honest retired major-general, while reading a novel in his club, to stop puzzling at one place for an hour or more in his bewilderment at this delightful trick, and for years after he would exclaim with admiration at the style of the writer.

The fourth canon of style is *to use metaphors* of a striking, violent, and wholly novel kind, in the place of plain statement: as, to say "the classics were grafted on the standing stirp of his mind rather than planted in its soil," which means that the man had precious little Greek, or again, "we propose to canalize, not to dam the current of Afghan development," which means that the commander of our forces in India strongly refused to campaign beyond the Khyber.

This method, which is invaluable for the purpose of flattering the rich, is very much used among the clergy, and had its origin in our great Universities, where it is employed to conceal ignorance, and to impart tone and vigour to the tedium of academic society. The late Bishop of Barchester was a past master of this manner, and so was Diggin, the war correspondent, who first talked of a gun "coughing" at one, and was sent home by Lord Kitchener for lying.

The fifth canon of style is, that when you are bored with writing and do not know what to say next, you should hint at unutterable depths of idea by the introduction of a row of asterisks.

* * * * * * *

THE ODE.

The writing of Odes seems to have passed so completely out of our literary life, that I thought it inadvisable to incorporate any remarks upon it with the standing part of my book, but I cannot refrain from saying a few words upon it in the Appendix, since I am convinced that it is destined to play a great part in the near future.

I will take for my example the well-known Ode (almost the only successful modern example of this form of composition) which was sung on the beach at Calshott Castle, by a selected choir, on the return of Mr. Joseph Chamberlain from South Africa; and I will use some passages from it in order to emphasize the leading principle that *the Ode depends for its effectiveness almost entirely upon the music accompanying it.*

Thus, Mr. Daniel Witton's opening lines:

> "What stranger barque from what imperial shores
> The angry Solent dares to what mysterious goal?"

would seem tame enough were it not for the wonderful rising of the notes, which accompany them; and the famous outburst:

> "She to Southampton steers!"

is equally dependent upon the crash of music and the combined voices of the whole choir. It is difficult for us, who have heard it rendered in the Albert Hall, to appreciate what the words would be without this adventitious aid. Even the lovely single line,

"Lift up your head, Southampton, dry your honourable tears,"

would be less without the delicate soprano floating above its syllables.

I will admit that the passage on the body-guard of National Scouts is very fine, but then, precisely in proportion as it is effective *quâ* literature, it fails to impress when accompanied by music, though the author of the score was wise enough to set it to a somewhat monotonous recitative. If the student will read the lines slowly to himself, first with, and then without, the notes, he will see what I mean.

"And who more fit than they
Whose better judgment led them to betray
An aged leader and a failing cause
Because —
Because they found it pay."

Mr. Daniel Witton did not write that word "because" twice over in his original manuscript. He put it in twice to please the musician (whose ignorance of the English tongue was a great handicap throughout), and, as I at least think, he made an error in so doing.

All that passage where the great politician

". . . taking off his hat,"

comes into the palace at Pretoria, where

". . . in awful state alone,
Alone, the scientific Monist sat,
Who guards our realm, extends its narrow bounds,
And to achieve his end,
Is quite prepared to spend
The inconceivably imperial sum of twice three hundred times five hundred thousand pounds,"

shows the grave difficulty of wedding the verse to the music. The last line is intolerably clumsy, when read without the air accompanying it; and the whole illustrates very well my contention that music should be the chief thing in the composition of an ode, and that the libretto should be entirely subservient to it.

A still better example is found in the great chorus "Pretoria," which begins—

> "Pretoria with her hundred towers
> Acknowledges his powers,"

and "Johannesburg," which ends—

> "Heil! heil! hoch! heil! du ubermenslich' wohl-gebornen Graf von Chamberlein,
> While underground,
> While underground,
> Such rare and scattered Kaffirs as are found
> Repeat the happy, happy, happy, happy sound."

And of course the lyric at the end—

> "All in his train de luxe
> Reading selected books,
> Including Conan Doyle's ingenious fiction
> And popular quota-
> Tions, verses by the way
> For which he has a curious predilection,
> And Mr. Werther's work
> Called 'England shall not shirk,'
> Or 'The Cape to Cairo, Kairouan and Cadiz,
> And 'Burke,' and 'Who is Who,'
> And 'Men and Women' too,
> And 'Etiquette for Gentlemen and Ladies,'"
> Et cetera, et cetera.

All that lyric depends entirely for its effects upon the little Venetian air taken from Sullivan, who himself took it from Verdi, who got it from a Gondolier. The words by themselves have no beauty whatsoever.

Indeed, I think in the whole Ode there is but one exception to the rule I have laid down, and that is at the very end, where they sing of the accomplished task and, in a fine hyperbole, of the "Great story that shall shake the affrighted years."

The last five lines are such good music and such good verse that I cannot dissociate one from the other:—

CHORUS. And now returns he, turns, turns he to his own—

TROMBONE. Ah, maddened with delight,
I welcome him upon the loud trombone.

THE BASS DRUM. I, in more subtle wise,
Upon the big bass drum.

THE TENOR. And I upon the trembling flute, that shrieks and languishes and dies.

ALL THREE. Welcome, and make a widowed land rejoice:
Welcome, attunéd voice;—
Sweet eyes!

It is a very fine ending, and I congratulate Mr. Daniel Witton upon it most sincerely. . . .

* * * * * *

It reminds one of the Bacchæ.

* * * * * *

Should the student desire to attempt something of the kind for himself, he cannot do better than to invite a musical friend and compose the ode strictly in conjunction with him; neither should write separately from the other, and let there be no quarrels or tantrums, but let each be ready to give way.

I suggest, as a subject for this exercise, a Funeral Ode upon the same statesman, to be sung when occasion serves.

ON REMAINDERS AND PULPING.

SHOULD the student aspire to collect his journalistic work, or the less ephemeral part of it, into book form, he will do well to apply to some old and established firm of publishers, who will give him a reasonable estimate for its production, plus the cost of advertising, warehousing, wear and tear, office expenses, etc., etc., to which must be added the customary Fee.

The book so issued will be sent to the Press for notice and review, and will, some weeks later, be either Remaindered or Pulped. It is important to have a clear idea of these processes which accompany an author throughout his career.

A book is said to be *Remaindered* when it is sold to the secondhand bookseller in bulk; 10 per cent. of the sums so received, less the cost of cartage to and fro from shop to shop, and the wages of the Persuader who attempts to sell the volumes, is then credited to the author in his account, which is usually pressed upon the completion of the transaction.

The less fortunate must be content with *Pulping.* In the midst of their chagrin they will be consoled by the thought that their book enjoys a kind of resurrection, and will reappear beneath some other, and—

who knows ?—perhaps some nobler form. The very paper upon which these words are printed may once have formed part of a volume of verse, or of Imperialist pamphlets subsidised by the South African Women's League.

A book is said to be *Pulped* when it is sold at so many pence the thousand copies to the Pulpers* for Pulping. The transformation is effected as follows:—First the covers are thoroughly and skilfully torn off the edition by girls known as "Scalpers" or "Skinners," and the Poems (or whatnot), after going through this first process, are shot in batches of twenty-four into a trough, which communicates by an inclined plane with open receptacles known technically as "bins." Hence the sheets are taken out by another batch of hands known as "feeders"—for it is their duty to "feed" the marvellous machine which is the centre of the whole works. The Poems (as we may imagine them to be) are next thrown by the "feeders," with a certain rapid and practised gesture, into a funnel-shaped receiver, where they are caught by Six Large Rows of strong Steel Teeth † known as the "Jaws," which are so arranged as just barely to miss each other; these work alternatively

* Messrs. Ibbotson, of Fetter-lane, and Charlton and Co., of St. Anne's, are the best-known Pulpers.

† Until Lord Balton (then Sir Charles Quarry) invented this part of the machine, poems, apologies for Christianity, &c., in fact all kinds of books, had to be torn laboriously into minute pieces by hand. It is difficult for us to realise now-a-days what exertion this involved. We live in an age of machinery!

back and forth, and reduce the hardest matter to shreds in an incredibly short time.

The shreds so formed fall on to a wide endless band, which carries them on into the "bowl," where they are converted under a continual stream of boiling water, into a kind of loose paste. Lest any trace of the original Poetic (or Prose) composition could remain to trouble the whiteness of the rapidly forming mixture, this water contains a 30% solution of Sardonic Oxide, two kilogrammes of which will bleach one thousand kilos of shredded Poems or Essays in from thirty-five to forty minutes. When the Poems or whatnot have been finally reduced to a white and formless mass, they are termed *pulp* and this pulp is laid out into frames, to be converted once more into paper, Art, glazed, and medium.

This principle of "the Conservation of Paper" or, as Lord Balton (Sir Charles Quarry) has himself called it, "the Circulation of Literature," is naturally more developed among the Anglo-Saxon peoples than upon the Continent. The patriotic reader will be pleased to hear that whereas of existing German books barely 35% are pulped within the year, of French books not 27%, and of Italian but 15%; of our total production—which is far larger—no less than 73% are restored to their original character of useful blank paper within the year, ready to receive further impressions of Human Genius and to speed on its accelerated round the progress of Mankind.

AMEN.

INDEX.

PRINTED BY R. FOLKARD AND SON,
22, DEVONSHIRE STREET, QUEEN SQUARE, BLOOMSBURY.

CPSIA information can be obtained
at www.ICGtesting.com
Printed in the USA
LVHW081507010621
689049LV00007B/167

9 780526 287079